You are
Whole, Perfect
and Complete...
JUST AS YOU ARE

compiled by
Carol Plummer and Susan Driscoll
FEATURING 12 AMAZING AUTHORS

Edited by Deborah Bowman Stevens
ClasidConsultantsPublishing.com

Cover Art by Mindy Wagner
Shakti Emerging by Mindy Wagner, 2014. Copyright Mindy Wagner.

ISBN-13: 978-0-9862480-0-9

Printed in the United States of America

Contents

Foreword

As Editors and Contributors, we searched for an appropriate opening to this wonderfully diverse collaborative work. Consequently, we agreed to begin this book in a unique fashion, with a channeled message. The Foreword comes from Martin, an entity who has chosen to teach higher wisdom and works through Susan. We hope you will enjoy his perspective on our book, "You Are Whole, Perfect, and Complete: Just as You Are."—Carol Plummer and Susan Driscoll

Message from Martin

"Thank you for this opportunity to set the tone for your collaborative work. This is indeed a time when this kind of information needs to be disseminated to the population.

For there is so much negativity; there is so much judgment; there is so much self-doubt. That it is important for all to remember that as human beings that you are creatures of the universe and that each and every one has within you the God source—that spark that makes you connected to universal source.

And in that way you, of course, are perfect. Humanity is perfection in the works. Perfection is not a state of total and complete stasis, it is a state of progression. So progression is always in-progress. And this we wish for people to understand, especially women. For women keep the flame of life burning. They take care of the hearth, the home; they are the true love energy that the planet experiences.

So, what we would say first and foremost is that women need to accept perfection. Even perfection in-progress and that in each moment there is another opportunity to improve upon that perfection. And when we say "to improve" we mean to say "expand, the perfection."

Perfection is quite a lovely state, and when you are embracing your perfection, you are acknowledging that you are one with source. And of course, there is no better place than to be one with source. So, now that you understand perfection, now we would like to discuss "whole." When you use the terminology "whole" we want you to imagine that it is the complete integration of the body, mind, and spirit.

There is not a separation of body, mind, and spirit, but a total integration of body, mind, and spirit. So in embracing this concept, remember that all of these aspects are integrated in the human experience and in the human light. There is no separation, and so you must love the emotional body that comes with the physical body. There is, of course, the energy body, and the mind in its perfection moves and inspires all aspects of an individual. So we see that this particular word we are looking for is the embracing of the integration of all that comprises humanity. And to remember it is in this integration, which these pieces move together in synchronicity.

And when we say that perfection is a work in-progress, it is all of these aspects working in-progress. It is not just we are going to work on our spiritual development and neglect everything else—we are going to work on having a better physical body and we neglect everything else. So, indeed it all works together.

And so, we come to the next word, which is "complete." Completion is a place where, as we say, you are a work in-progress at this moment. Your progress is complete until the next moment when it is complete again, and the next moment and so on.

Remember that completion, like being perfect, is a work in-progress, and it moves in synchronicity with body, mind, and spirit. So, the concept of this book is to remind those that "just the way you are" in this moment is perfection and is beauty. And it moves forward with all body, mind, spirit, and working together to say "that I am in this moment complete. And I am in this moment of perfection. And I am in this moment expanding to the next moment," where this will be moving, yet again into another energetic place. So, it is quite a lovely concept.

We wish for everyone who reads this to be inspired to understand that this is all about humanity embracing the moment, and humanity embracing its perfection, embracing its completion, embracing all of its parts and seeing that this comes together in each and every human being.

And it is indeed in each and every human being, and it is to be celebrated. It is to be celebrated for in this world some say there is so much darkness; we say "there's so much light." There is so much beauty in so much grace. For when all of this comes together in the conscious mind you see that there is a state of grace—a state of connection to source. And that is indeed what all on the planet strives for. So we say "to be all perfect and complete just the way you are" is indeed a concept that is beautiful, that is deeply spiritual, and that brings the human experience to its pinnacle."

Loving Yourself

Carol Plummer

What is your relationship with yourself? How do you treat yourself? Are you loving toward yourself or do you treat yourself poorly? Do you feel good about whom you are, or do you feel unworthy or not good enough? Do you beat yourself up? What is the running commentary in your head, your self-talk? Is it positive and supportive? Or negative and self-denigrating?

When I first started thinking about self-love, I became aware of how self- critical I had become. My commentary included phrases like, "*Why did I say that? How could I have done that? How could I do something so stupid! Why didn't I...*" In fact, I remember waking up one morning haranguing myself about something I failed to do. It didn't make any sense since I didn't do it, and it was too late to correct it. Why continue to feel guilty? I finally let it go, but it was amazing how hard I was on myself. This energized the topic for me and put me on the path to improve my own level of self-love and appreciation which I now want to share with you.

Why don't we love ourselves? I believe there are lots of reasons. Our society and culture has conditioned us to believe we are not okay. Our puritan culture of self-sacrifice leads us to feel that others are more worthy than ourselves. This idea that we should *give until it hurts* says that others deserve our blood, sweat, and tears more than we do.

1

Many religions make us feel guilty with the concept of sin, starting with original sin, which we are supposedly born with. It is difficult to love ourselves if we are sinners. My religious upbringing was Catholic where nuns and priests, who took vows of poverty and chastity, were the ultimate and exalted role models of service to others and good human beings. As a child, how could I love myself when compared to these role models? I believed that I was selfish, self-centered, and flawed. I perceived that I didn't deserve to love myself. What did the religious tradition you were raised in teach you about yourself?

The idea that *"we are not good enough"* is pervasive in our culture. Consider the media that says we can make our lives better if we buy products X, Y, and Z, implying that we are not okay or worthwhile without these name brands. Our schools and teachers with varied and competitive grading systems are designed to ensure that we are kept in-line and criticized for our own good. The supposition is that we must be judged and chastised to fit into our society's view of a good person. These structures tend to be hard on anyone who is different or unique. As our uniqueness is judged and critiqued, we question our value and worth. In light of this, is it not surprising that we find it hard to love ourselves?

Another influence is our family. How did your family treat you? If our family, who is supposed to love us unconditionally, can't love us; how can we love ourselves? I remember an incident from my childhood. I was about 13 and my family was going out to dinner. I had fixed my hair, pulling the front back with a barrette exposing my ears. I thought it was sophisticated, but my father looked at me and said, *"You look ridiculous with your ears sticking out."* I was deflated; I felt rejected and ugly; it destroyed my self-confidence which at that age was already tenuous. My conclusion was that I was not worthy of love because if my father couldn't love me how could I love myself? To this day I don't wear my hair in any way that shows my ears! If your family was negative and belittling, it made it hard for you to appreciate your worth and love yourself.

Yet loving ourselves is so important to our self-confidence and sense of self-worth. If we have a low sense of self-esteem, it's harder to make friends and maintain good relationships. We find it difficult to believe that someone else could love us because we feel we don't deserve love. And if we don't believe that they truly love us, we can't return their love. Friendships and intimate relationships require mutual respect, appreciation, and the reciprocity of love. If we can't respect and appreciate ourselves, we question that someone else can respect and love us and, therefore, question and doubt the other person's feelings. This can lead to mistrust and an eventual breakdown of the relationship. Another aspect of not valuing ourselves is when we suspect others of not appreciating us. We, in turn, question their value and worth as well... *"Anyone that loves and values "me" must not be somebody worth knowing!"*

"If you aren't good at loving yourself, you will have a difficult time loving anyone, since you'll resent the time and energy you give another person that you aren't even giving to yourself."
Barbara De Angelis

What is Self-Love?

I believe self-love is about self-acceptance, respect, and appreciating myself just as I am. Loving myself is about appreciating who I am right now, who I have been, and who I will become. It's about being okay with myself, no matter what. It's about unconditional acceptance. The more I can accept and just be *"me,"* the more I am loving myself.

Loving yourself is about valuing your unique combination of characteristics, abilities, and flaws. It's about being good to yourself by taking care of yourself mentally, physically, emotionally, and spiritually. It's about being yourself and sharing who you are with others. Sharing your gifts with the world is how you make a difference in the world. This sharing and personal giving presence leads to success. Self-love is also the key to happiness. You cannot be happy unless you're true to yourself.

> *"Accept your humanness as well as your divinity,*
> *totally and without reserve."*
> **Emmanuel**

Sandra Yancey, CEO of eWomen Network, says, *"For me, self-love is having an honest, honoring, compassionate, forgiving and fulfilling relationship with yourself. It's easy to describe yet challenging to do."*

According to Wikipedia: *"Self-love is the love of oneself…"* and further explains, *"…that Erich Fromm proposed that loving oneself means caring about oneself, taking responsibility for oneself, respecting oneself, and knowing oneself (e.g., being realistic and honest about one's strengths and weaknesses)."*

Can you love yourself too much? If we define self-love as we have in this chapter with terms such as appreciation, values, forgiveness, and fulfillment, then it is not possible to love ourselves too much. On the other hand, narcissism, egotism, and arrogance are not attributes of self-love. These are the opposite of self-love, creating negative aspects of self-grandeur and self-illusion. We may want to look at what we are doing and becoming if these traits become noticeable to yourself or others. These obsessive feelings can lead to psychological disorders. Loving ourselves can only make us better human beings with feelings of happiness and success!

You might be thinking, *"…but I need to constantly criticize myself to make myself better!"* Actually the opposite is true. Kristen Neff, in her book "Self-Compassion: Stop Beating Yourself Up and Leave Insecurity Behind," says, *"When you make mistakes or fall short of your expectations, you can throw away that rawhide whip and instead throw a cozy blanket of compassion around your shoulders. You will be more motivated to learn, grow, and make the much needed changes in your life, while also having more clarity to see where you are now and where you'd like to go next. You'll have the security needed to go after what you really want as well as the support and encouragement necessary to fulfill your dreams."*

I love this idea of a *"…cozy blanket of compassion around your shoulders."* If you are challenged to do this for yourself, the best strategy I have found when I do something that I judge was not perfect and am struggling to be self-compassionate is to ask myself if one of my friends did what I did, what would I say to them? Several months ago I forgot to include some information that I had promised would be in the newsletter. I started to go to the place of berating myself with, "How could I have done something so stupid and irresponsible?" I caught myself and asked, *"What would I tell my friend if they were sharing this mistake?"* And I realized that I would tell that friend, *"It's okay…stuff happens; you can include it next month."* Consider how you can use this strategy to be more compassionate to yourself.

How do we become more self-loving and compassionate? First, we must recognize that loving and believing in ourselves is an attitude and a choice. So, step one is to decide that you are going to be more kind and loving to yourself. Now, how do you do that? One way is with self-compassion. According to Kristen Neff there are three steps or components: mindfulness, recognition of our common humanity, and being kind to ourselves. By using these steps we can stop self-criticism in its tracks and start being more compassionate. The first step, mindfulness, is about awareness. It is learning to watch and become aware of our thoughts and feelings. The idea is to be present in the moment and know what you are saying to yourself and feeling. One way to do this is to ask yourself, *"What am I thinking?"* or *"What am I feeling right now?"* As you become aware and identify the feelings, name them… *"I feel sad, disappointed, confused, curious…etc."* Then, breathe into the feelings. As we become aware and label our feelings, we gain control of them, reducing their power over us.

The 2nd step is the recognition of our common humanity. It doesn't matter whether you caused your suffering or not. We are all beings having a human experience, and we make mistakes and suffer. It is part of our human experience, and everyone is part of it. Let yourself appreciate the connection and recognize that everyone is having similar experiences. You can say to yourself, *"It's okay. Everyone makes mistakes. No one's perfect."*

> *"If it is a virtue to love my neighbor as a human being, it must be a virtue—and not a vice—to love myself, since I am a human being too."*
> **Erich Fromm**

The 3rd step is to be kind to yourself. This means treating yourself gently. It includes not just letting go of self-criticism and judgment, but actively comfort and soothe yourself. This could be stroking yourself or giving yourself a hug by wrapping your arms around yourself and squeezing. Saying supportive and comforting words like, *"Everything is OK...I love you...It always works out...Things will get better."*

> *"You yourself, as much as anybody in the entire universe, deserve your love and affection."*
> **Buddha**

Ways to Love Yourself

Since loving yourself is critical to your health, let's talk about ways we can love ourselves with happiness and success. Here are ten strategies to love yourself or love yourself more. Try them and tell me how they work for you.

1. An easy first step to loving yourself is to love and nurture your body. This means treating it well and taking care of it. Your body is your vehicle...your temple for existing on the earth. It is the only one you have. If you abuse it...you will lose it. By nurturing our bodies we are telling ourselves that we are worthwhile and have value. Treating our bodies well includes feeding it healthy, nutritious foods; keeping it in shape; getting enough sleep and maintaining it. Advanced nurturing could be spa days, massage, acupuncture, reflexology...whatever makes you physically feel good.

2. Identify what you like, love, and appreciate about yourself. Cristi Cook, Kelley Edelblut, and I created this simple exercise for "A Better Balanced You Workshop." It may be done by yourself or with a partner. The most effective execution is to speak it out loud. If you are doing it by yourself, you may write them out. For one minute say, *"What I love about myself is..."* Then for one minute say, *"What I appreciate about myself is..."* Then for one minute say, *"What I like about myself is..."* If you write them down, you may read them over to remind yourself what a wonderful person you are and boost your confidence.

3. Treat yourself like you would a best friend. Here's how I would treat a good friend: Try not to hurt their feelings; you want them to be happy; listen to them; respect their feelings, and opinions; and appreciate them for who they are, just as they are (foibles and all). A good friend would be supportive and compassionate towards you. If you shared with them some mistake or bad situation...what would their response be? It would be understanding, kind and forgiving. Wouldn't they help you put the incident into perspective, saying things like... *"In the big picture how important was what you did/what happened? It is okay and will work out. You can do better next time."* They might help you see what triggered the response or reaction and determine if you should do something to change your relationship or the situation. They would be compassionate and on your side...loving you for who you are.

4. Set boundaries. As you begin to love yourself, decide how you want to be treated. As Sonya Friedman says, *"The way you treat yourself sets the standard for others."* How we treat ourselves tells people how to treat us. The more you respect yourself, the more others will respect you. The other aspect of boundaries is how you give. Many of us with self-worth issues are people-pleasers. We think if we give enough, they will love us…not realizing that we must love ourselves first. As we give and give we resent it, feel taken advantage of, and get burned out. The strategy for serving is a concept I learned from Lisa Nichols, which is to serve from your saucer. So you fill-up your cup until it overflows and serve from this excess. This ensures that you are giving from abundance, which leads to greater self-respect.

5. Visualizations and meditations are wonderful tools for changing our mindset and training our minds and egos. Here is one on loving yourself (A free recording is available for download on the www.youarewholeperfectandcomplete.com website):

Meditation for Loving Yourself

Get comfortable and
Take some deep breaths…
Notice how your body feels…your feet flat on the floor…your hands comfortably in your lap
As you breathe feel the air flowing in and out of your nostrils
Gently breathe in calm and exhale tension, letting any tightness or discomfort flow out of your body
Bring to mind some mistake you made, or a self-judgment or an inadequacy or lack
Get in touch with the feelings thinking about this…do you feel sad, isolated, disappointed, annoyed or some other emotion? Allow the feelings…whatever they are…they are what they are

Now, put your hand to your heart…sense your heart…can your heart be moved by these emotions and sufferings? You try your best but we are all imperfect. Feel the compassion your heart has for you.

Say to yourself:
May I be safe.
May I be peaceful.
May I be kind to myself.
May I accept myself as I am.

Feel the warmth of your hand on your heart…feel the intention of these phrases and let yourself experience them…
May I be safe.
May I be peaceful.
May I be kind to myself.
May I accept myself as I am.

Everyone has imperfections and inadequacies…let's include all these people in our mantra.
May we be safe.
May we be peaceful.
May we be kind to ourselves.
May we accept ourselves as we are.

Feel in your heart core tenderness, love and connection. Thank yourself for opening your heart and being compassionate to yourself and others and know that you can do this at any time.

Bring your awareness to your body as you take some deep breaths… feel your body and slowly bring yourself and your compassionate heart back to the present…open your eyes when you are ready.

6. Eliminate negative beliefs. What are beliefs? Beliefs are premises or thoughts that we believe to be true. Beliefs are thoughts we keep thinking. If we remember the Law of Attraction, whatever we keep thinking will come into our experience. So, beliefs are patterns of thinking that will determine what we are experiencing in our lives. The problem with beliefs is that we often don't realize that we have them. They are transparent to us. They are such a part of our mental operating system that we are not able to determine that they are impacting our lives by filtering what we are seeing. I think Maurice Chapman summarizes it nicely:

    "All of us, throughout our lives, develop and adopt systems of beliefs about the world we are living in. While our specific beliefs may be fluid, our set of beliefs at any given time, shapes how we interpret and process each experience and moment. As such, it acts as a filter through which we perceive and observe."

    We can change what we are thinking if we know what we are thinking. So, what are your beliefs about yourself? We are going to do an exercise that will let you examine some of them and whether they are helpful or not.

    Write the answers to the following on paper:

    What are three beliefs you have about yourself?
    What are three beliefs about yourself; how you are in the world?
    What are three beliefs about your body?
    What are three beliefs about loving yourself?
    Now, for each of the beliefs you listed...which are supportive or helpful and which are hindering or detrimental? Write an S if it supportive or H if it is hindering or detrimental.

    For those that have an H (Hindering), rewrite the belief so that it is positive. It may the opposite of something that will counteract the negative belief. So, if the detrimental belief was, "It's hard to love my-self." Then the rewrite could be, "It's easy to love myself," or "Loving myself is easy." Affirming these new beliefs for several days or weeks will anchor them into your psyche, replacing the old negative beliefs. (See next step on affirmations.)

7. Create and practice positive self-talk through affirmations re-placing negative self-talk and thoughts. Affirmations are positive statements repetitively vocalized to create a change in thought and/or behavior. Gandhi said, *"What we think we become."* By changing our thoughts we can change what we are and do. To *affirm* some-thing is simply to declare that it is true.

Affirmations are a very powerful tool for creating. Repetition of positive statements until those thoughts become a natural part of the way you think, act to crowd out, and replace the negative thought patterns you have been sending all these years. To create powerful affirmations, include the following:

Content = *outcome* you desire. Emotion = how you *feel* about it:

1. Present tense "now"
2. Be positive (skip the word "not")
3. Be concise
4. Include action
5. Include a feeling word

Research indicates: With positive self-talk + visualization + train-ing and practice, anyone can learn to do almost anything. Put aside your doubt and fear…practice, practice, practice…

Breathe, relax, focus on the feeling, repeat multiple times daily.

Some examples for believing in yourself:

"I am healthy, wealthy, and wise. Things always work out for me. I am happy to be me. I accomplish my goals easily. I am a powerful, resourceful creator. I am confident, capable, and connected. I am happy where I am." (My personal favorites.)

"I approve of myself. I am worthy of love. I am smart and make wise choices. I am loveable and capable. I am able to solve any problem that comes my way. I am successful. I attract all the right people into my life. I love my life. I am happy and healthy."—Cristi Cook, ABBY

"I accept myself unconditionally. I love myself as I am. I forgive myself. I am being what love is guiding me to be."—Rev. Dr. Patrick Cameron.

"I am my own best friend, filled with self-kindness and self-compassion. I treat myself gently as I learn and grow, knowing I'm worthy of every happiness."—Rev. Jane Beach

Repetition of the affirmation to replace old programming (beliefs and thoughts) may be done through vocalization, reading, feeling, thinking, writing, and visualization or a combination. The more modes utilized the easier it is to achieve the change you desire. Choose to believe that you can and you will.

8. Forgive yourself. Sometimes it is hard to love ourselves because we have done something(s) that we feel are unforgiveable. First, forgiving is a choice. If the guilt and shame are deep, then we need more than the decision to let go and forgive ourselves. There are many processes you can use. The key steps in most processes involve telling and acknowledging the story, experiencing and healing the feelings/wounds, reframing the story/experience, and then integrating and moving forward. The two (slightly different steps

but same result) I am familiar with are Radical Forgiveness by Colin Tipping www.radicalforegiveness.com and The Forgiveness Option by Harry Palmer, author of the Avatar materials http://www.avatarepc.com/html/Pillar5-Forgiveness-Eng.pdf. Check out the websites for free material and more information.

9. Let yourself be you. You can love yourself by accepting who you are without excuses or exception. This acceptance is about making peace and appreciating who we are just as we are and loving ourselves no matter what we are doing or feeling. Our feelings and behavior are not who we are but manifestations of a situation or belief. They can be changed and we can love ourselves regardless. Consider the idea that we are spiritual beings having a human experience and as spiritual beings, we are whole, perfect and complete. We can appreciate and support our human experience as it is our way to grow and learn.

   Consider the idea that you are the unique manifestation of you. Only you are the essence of you...unique, perfect, and whole just as you are. Why shouldn't you love you? Louise Hay says it nicely:

   "In the infinity of life where I am, All is perfect, whole and complete, I no longer choose to believe in old limitations and lack, I now choose to begin to see myself...As the Universe sees me—perfect, whole, and complete."

10. Identify positive aspects of yourself. Another exercise you can do when you feel a need to shift from a negative view of yourself to a more positive perspective is to ask yourself these questions or complete these statements (you can write or journal them):

    - *What's special and unique about me? These are your special skills or qualities.*
    - *People tell me they're amazed I can...(fill in the blank).*

- *I'm really good at...(fill in the blank). It may be hard to admit it because we don't usually brag about what we are great at.*
- *No one else seems to be able to...(fill in the blank)...like I can. Hint: What do other people come to you to do because they can't or they are not as good as you are?*

You can write these down in a journal or on a notecard and refer to these notes for a boost to your self-loving and confidence.

In conclusion, I leave you with the words of Thadeus Golas, philosopher, who wrote:

"Whatever you are doing, love yourself for doing it. Whatever you are feeling, love yourself for feeling it."

"Namaste."

Carol Plummer is the Executive Managing Director of the Montgomery County, MD chapter of eWomenNetwork and CEO of Spirituality for Every Day. eWomenNetwork is the premiere resource for connecting and promoting women and their businesses and is dedicated to supporting, promoting and showcasing members' products and services and helping them achieve their professional objectives. For more information go to www.ewomennetwork.com/chapter/montgomery

The vision for Spirituality for Every Day is a world where everyone feels centered, peaceful and connected to their spirituality. The mission is to provide tools and experiences that enables people to achieve our vision. For more information go to www.spiritualityforeveryday.com

Prior to her current positions Carol was the cofounder of A Better Balanced You whose mission was to provide services for women to increase the joy, peace and happiness in their lives, an entrepreneur for 5 years with a jewelry business and teacher of a self improvement course and a 30 year corporate career with a large computer company.

Embrace Your Gifts

Susan Q. Driscoll, M.A.

It is a rather curious thing to be an intuitive channel and medium. You can't get a degree in channeling. There are no formal schools to train you; there are no certificate programs to verify your expertise. You can't really go to "Career Day" with your elementary school aged child and explain what you do. Cocktail party conversation comes to a screeching halt when you respond to a stranger's rather perfunctory, *"What do you do?"* inquiry. Try putting it on your tax return as your occupation, for example. It sends the accountants and the IRS into orbit!

There are no professional organizations for channels and mediums, no American Association of Channels and Mediums, with dues and annual conventions. There are no "Continuing Education Units," no workbooks, no professional development requirements or seminars. It is, as I stated, a rather unique occupation, shrouded in mystery and skepticism. It is certainly an isolating profession—there are no group practices of channels, such as "Smith and Jones, Channeling and Mediumship, LLC."

Oh, and did I mention that you do your work in an altered state? A channel and/or medium surrenders her conscious experience to allow alternate energies to work through her. All things considered, who, indeed, would want to pursue that line of work?

That question had been posed to my daughter recently, which got me to thinking about who I am and what I do. I believe the exact words were, *"Why would Susan want to go down that path?"* The implication, of course being that *"down that path"* was a choice. And, that choice was a very sketchy one, made by someone who should know better.

Right, I should know better. On paper, I look very traditional, very established, a very seasoned professional in a respected career. I am by training, a licensed counselor. I have done both career counseling and psychotherapy. In my traditional career, I have worked in agencies, academia, and private practice. Why would I choose to be a channel and a medium? The answer is quite simple. It is not a choice. It is who I am. It is a gift that I was born with, one that is as much a part of me as my green eyes, my smile, and my 5' 7" frame.

And, it is a gift that I spent decades denying. Those years of denial were exhausting and confusing, leaving me feeling like I was living a double life. There was my public persona, and then there was that other, more private person. You know, that private person who could do some pretty weird things that were not part of your everyday experience. Not everyone has a daily calendar that reads: grocery shopping, cycle class, pick up dry cleaning, channeling session with Sal. It is because I led that double life, and suffered the consequences of it, that I chose to title this chapter, "Embrace Your Gifts."

Now that I have moved out of my "double life" and into the open, I find that the dialogue with the uninitiated is exciting and stimulating. Imagine my surprise when I realized that I was not being treated as a side-show attraction, but as a respected and valued teacher, a source of higher wisdom when conventional wisdom falls short of supplying answers or a better perspective.

We are all unique and wonderful beings, blessed with gifts and challenges that create the rich fabric of our lives. Like many intuitives, I had psychic experiences as a young child that were totally discounted by my family members. As a result, I was very shy and introverted. I read a great deal and was especially attracted to church and the study of religion. This was a big plus for me, since I was sent to Catholic schools from first grade through college.

On my twenty-first birthday, my roommate Ann gave me the Eden Gray deck of Tarot cards and an instruction book. And so, I began my adventure in developing my intuition. I enjoyed learning about the cards, their meanings, and different ways to create readings. I also noticed that the more I used the cards, the more information I was receiving, telepathically. It wasn't a voice in my ear or an angel appearing before me, it was simply a "knowing," an understanding that information was coming to me from another source.

This was fun; it was different; and it was definitely a parlor game. I did not take it seriously, even though the information was accurate and surprised many who had "a reading." This was just a hobby, something for entertainment, nothing more. I was safe; I was normal.

It was about that time, in my mid-twenties, when I began to read more about metaphysical matters. I became friendly with members of a spiritual community and began to attend some of the classes that were offered. I learned about chakras, Atlantis, spirit guides, life on the "other side," and reincarnation, to name a few topics. I began to understand that there is a whole other dimension to life, well beyond our three-dimensional, physical reality. I was intrigued and became an excellent student, soaking up as much knowledge as I could. I found each and every topic fascinating.

I also started to have very vivid dreams, precognitive dreams. And, it became a rite of passage that every person in my family who died and crossed over contacted me, letting me know that they were safely on "the other side." I developed the very bad habit of finishing other people's sentences and seeing their auras. Talk about an invasion of privacy!

So, this is when I developed a pattern that would serve me for the next fifteen years. I would read, take a class, play with my cards, have my dreams and my precognitions. Then I would discount it all and return to my "normal" life. I enjoyed these activities, but again, it was just a hobby, just entertainment. I had no desire to be one of those weirdoes . . . I just wanted to be a normal person with a normal life. I was denying who I was. I was far from embracing my gifts. I was rejecting them. I wanted nothing to do with the whole idea of accepting that I was an intuitive. But, as the expression goes, *"We make plans and the gods laugh."*

Well, you really can't run away from you. You can change the scenery around you, move to a new location, change jobs, get new friends. You can gain weight, lose weight, straighten your hair, color your hair, buy new clothes, find new shoes, pierce your ears, pierce your nose, tattoo your body up one side and down the other. The truth is that all you are doing is changing the external scenery—you are not changing who you are and what you bring to the table.

As a counselor, I have worked with many clients over the years who say, *"This is who I am. I can't change."* The distinction I would make here is that we cannot change our very core, the essence of who we are. What we can change is how we think, how we respond, and how we behave. This is the foundation of counseling, a field dedicated to helping people create and maintain positive changes in their lives. A competent counselor will recognize the strengths a client has and work with that client to capitalize on those strengths.

One thing that is so very important for an individual to recognize is that self-awareness is the key to self-appreciation. Unfortunately, many of us are running around in our lives at a frantic pace, not allowing ourselves the time to explore our innermost selves. We are so caught up in a lifestyle that robs us of our leisure time and places unrealistic demands on our energy. We work; we raise families; we are involved with our communities; we workout at the gym; we drive carpools to soccer games and ballet practice; we cook; we clean; we keep up with our reading; we play tennis; we know everything that's going on in the world; we keep up with technology . . . the list can go on and on. We believe that we have to keep up with everything or we are somehow failures as human beings.

So, how do we become self-aware? It takes time; it takes courage; and it takes commitment. Let's look at those three parts:

Time . . . is so precious, and sometimes we feel that there is just not enough time in a day. Giving yourself the gift of time for self-exploration is so important to your growth as a human being. Block off some time each day to sit quietly without distractions. Find a practice in prayer/meditation/contemplation that works for you. And, when I say *"works for you,"* I mean just that. Don't be seduced into some long, involved practice that is difficult and uncomfortable for you. Start with something simple and build on it. Once you have found "your practice," stick to it, just like you would stick to a regular exercise program or a regular bedtime routine. Going within quietly and listening to your inner voice is essential in your adventure of self-exploration.

A word of advice—you will not necessarily hear a booming voice giving you specific directions. Nor will there be a thunderbolt coming down from the heavens, announcing a major change in your life. It is a quiet prompting from the heart that will move you. Move you to a level of deeper understanding of self. I cannot emphasize enough the need for daily quiet time, however you wish to express it. It soothes; it calms; it strengthens the soul. It gives perspective to life.

Courage . . . is our second step. Often, when we think of courage, we think of a very physical action. We think of soldiers on the battlefield, displaying valor during war. We think of cancer patients, undergoing severe treatments to heal the body. We think of leaders who make bold decisions to take their countries in a new direction. We think of the abused standing up to the abuser. We see these people in these kinds of situations as being full of courage. But we never think of ourselves as being courageous.

Courage comes in many different sizes, colors, and flavors. The examples I just gave are how we typically think of courage. We see it primarily as a physical action, one associated with many risks. But courage can also be a very cerebral activity. Courage to examine who you really are is not an easy task. It is a process of observing without judgment what you are made of and where you fall short. Going into that quiet place and noticing what's there, and what is not, is not for the faint of heart. The real trick here is to look, to assess, and NOT to judge.

Developing that internal self-awareness fosters the growth of courage. It is a certainty of where your moral compass will take you, without hesitation, no matter what the consequences. Courage understands that risks and consequences are all a part of life. And, a life worth living well always involves having the courage of one's convictions and allowing the chips to fall where they may.

Again, I go back to that basic premise of self-awareness that is so essential to all of us in life. And, when I look at my own experience, I now understand that I was blocking my own self-awareness by denying my gifts, and consequently, denying who I really was. I did not have the courage to see who I really was for many, many years. I had glimpses of it, but I failed to give it full credibility because I did not dig deeper into my psyche. I was caught up in public judgment, or what I perceived was public judgment. What an unfortunate loss of time and a waste of a beautiful gift. Fortunately, we are never too old to learn, to grow, to move forward.

Commitment . . . our third part of this discussion. . . puts the energy into the process. We have all heard the expression, *"You can't just talk the talk; you have to walk the walk."* And so, commitment is the walk of life. What really keeps us from making commitments? Or, if we do make commitments, why are they sometimes so difficult for us to keep those commitments?

Commitments are actions, and they are real. Once you make a commitment, your word is now transformed into action. It is there for all the world to see, to experience. And, of course, there's that word again, RISK. There is always a risk in putting yourself out there, in full view, for all the world to see. And so, many of us bargain with commitment, trading off bits and pieces so we feel more in control of the situation. Some of us will make commitments and go full-tilt. Others of us will proceed cautiously, timidly, into the realm of commitment. It really doesn't matter how you go into commitment, no matter what your pace, once you are there, you are there. And you are accountable, one hundred percent, for that to which you are committed.

Let's take a gut-check on this one. Where is your self-awareness about your ability to make a commitment and follow through? If commitment is a stumbling block for you, my best advice is to start small and work your way up to larger actions. Select just one thing, or a part of one thing, and make a commitment to take action. I can confess that this was how I proceeded in making my way to embracing my gifts. I could not look at the entire picture—it was just too large, too overpowering. So, I made a commitment to a first baby step in bringing my true self out into the world.

I remember that for the first few years of my channel opening, only one other person was aware of my capabilities, my dear friend, Anna. Anna was a "safe" person because she herself was an intuitive and understood my fears about being judged and ostracized. She helped me open the channel and gave me the confidence to continue exploring this gift. Over time, I then very cautiously disclosed to a few close friends my capabilities. I had to have the courage and the commitment to disclose and allow the reactions to happen. Most were excited, a few were dismissive, and yes, a few went screaming from the room.

Moving out into a more public forum came with time. Individual sessions turned into group sessions. Working from my home turned into working from my office, to working in other venues in a variety of locations. The word spread, I could no longer contain this gift in a tidy little box. It was no longer a hobby, no longer a pastime. It wasn't just something that I did, it was who I was. Couldn't turn it off if I wanted to, could no longer run away from it. Commitment had taken root and was growing.

Now that we have examined self-awareness, we are ready to take that next natural step and come to a place of self0appreciation. When we have taken the time, found our courage, and made our commitment, we are experiencing total self-awareness. Now for the icing on the cake, self-appreciation. Being aware is a state of acceptance, being appreciative is a state of celebration. It is a place where you truly acknowledge who you are and what you bring to the planet. And you rejoice in who you are!

This is where our book title comes into play: "You are Whole, Perfect, and Complete: Just as You Are." What a beautiful statement of self-appreciation and celebration. In this place, you understand that you are a unique being, put on this planet for a specific purpose. Reflect on all that you have done, all you have touched, all of the joy and encouragement that you have spread. Remember that when you feel you have fallen short, it is only because you are learning. Life is a process of learning, of growing, of finding our footing. There can be no growth without taking risks, and sometimes, risk teaches us different lessons than what we imagined would manifest as outcomes.

I have spoken of being a channel and a medium. I would now like to share with you some of my channeled wisdom on this topic of embracing your gifts. I have been fortunate to work with Martin, an ancient energy that brings information from the universal source. Martin is a teacher and a guide. Here are some of his thoughts on the topic of embracing your gifts:

"Embracing your gifts is a critical and integral part of being human. It is the most important task humans can engage in during any incarnation

and no matter what the circumstances. Gifts are part of the package we call humanity.

Each and every person on this planet has a gift or has several gifts. Each person, by virtue of the fact that they have incarnated, has contracted with universal source and with their higher selves to accept and embrace these gifts. They have agreed to fully and completely utilize these gifts to the best of their human capabilities.

Now, often, humans get a little bit confused. They believe these gifts should be beautifully wrapped, with elegant paper, and sparkles and bows. They should be neatly left by the doorstep amid much fanfare and unwrapped with great excitement. This is not always the case. Sometimes the gifts are delivered to the back door, or perhaps you have to find them hiding in the bushes, or where the UPS person has dropped them off. They may be in plain brown wrappers, or they may not look like gifts at all. They may look like something quite ordinary, or they might look like something that one might say is a challenge.

Let us talk about this. For this is truly the nugget we wish to emphasize: that gifts are not always readily apparent. They are not always beautifully wrapped. Sometimes they come in a cloak that the human mind perceives to be a challenge, or a nuisance, or an annoyance. Think about it. Let us use this example. When there is a stray cat that appears at the door. The stray cat is fed outside, but keeps coming back, and finally the cat is allowed inside the house and is adopted by the family. And, oh it is such a nuisance. More visits to the vets, more cat food to buy, more mess to clean up, cat fur and all this scratching on the furniture. What a nuisance.

Then this cat creeps into your lap, then this cat licks your face. The cat purrs and snuggles warmly against you, and then this cat keeps your feet warm at night. And then this cat looks at you with the eyes of wisdom, with the eyes of a gentle pure being when you are heart broken, when you are despondent, when you are in pain. This little cat offers you unconditional love. This scrawny little thing that appeared at the front door begging for food, all dirty and matted, is truly a gift.

And so, in this discussion of embracing your gifts we must first acknowledge that gifts are sometimes disguised. But nonetheless, they are gifts from Source. Each and every one of you has gifts. So do not judge from the externals, but with the internals, look at how this gift has made you grow, look at how this gift has made you a stronger person. You are a wiser person, more full of love, more full of caring and compassion, more alive, experiencing life, experiencing all aspects of life.

Allow yourself that full experience and embrace it. Embrace it with all of your heart, for it is what makes you whole, perfect, and complete. It's what makes you who you are and what allows you fully and completely to be a magnificent creature, that stands before you in the mirror. Embracing is the active celebration of allowing the gift. It is the active art of saying I wish to fully and completely experience this, without any reservation.

That is when you know, you are truly a child of God. You have truly transcended the human experience. When you have truly felt that this is why you are here, and you are here for the entire world to see. Not just for you, not just for an invitation-only audience. But, for an audience as far and as large as the cosmos, as deep and as wide as god source."

"Thank you, Martin!"

———•◦●◦•———

Susan Q. Driscoll, M.A., is a practicing intuitive channel, counselor and teacher. Susan holds a master's degree in counseling psychology and has worked as both a career and psychosocial counselor in agency and academic environments.

After many years of metaphysical searching and study, Susan began working with "Martin" energy in 1995. She conducts group and private channeling sessions, specializing in Akashic (past life) readings and life transition issues.

One of the strengths Susan brings to her spiritual practice is a real world grounded experience. Bridging the two worlds is her specialty, and she has helped many understand their intuitive gifts and how to integrate those gifts into daily life. Sessions are held in a relaxed environment, with respect for the individual's sensitivities and needs.

Currently Susan's private practice is located in Montgomery Village, Maryland, a Washington DC suburb. In her work, she integrates intuitive channeling, counseling and teaching. Susan has traveled and held channeling sessions in various parts of the country, and is also accessible for phone consultations.

Susan may be reached at www.martinsmessages.com or 301.977.4536

Your Joyous Path To Purpose

"You are a precious GEM: Unique, rare and valuable."

Bonnie Gordon Patterino

You are a G.E.M. (*Guided Energetic Messenger*) of truth, love, joy, and freedom, and you are here, perfectly created, to live a fulfilling life of purpose. You are a spiritual *being* of energetic frequency with a vibrating, emotional heart and a loving voice of powerful intention and meaningful spoken word. You were born into an amazing physical body with unique skills, rare personal *gifts*, valuable intellectual abilities to develop and use, and the unlimited potential to deeply understand yourself and the world.

Your more radiant beauty, like a diamond in the rough, shines most brightly from within. This hidden inner beauty and your purpose gifts will come forth as you dig deeply enough to mine them out and see the true value of your own self-worth. If you are brave enough and care enough to dive into that realm of self-discovery, you will be rewarded with an overflowing abundance of truth, love, joy, and freedom in your life.

True life transformation results in permanent shifts of positive change that created passionate desire, inspired motivation, and amplified ability to live out your *destiny*. This process of creating and contributing your beautiful gifts in order to help others is part of a larger purpose that helps the world. By daring to dig deeper, your potential to self-actualize a life of fulfillment, absolute joy, and personal freedom with infectious positive impact is limitless!

You are limitless and your eternal voice living inside, as *"born-wisdom,"* cannot be denied. It is impossible not to be on your purpose path because you have arrived with an inner guide (soul, higher self, inner voice, intuitive knowing, and divine connection to source energy) that has been naturally leading you all throughout your life. Having this living body and eternal soul working together, you are on a continual, living, eternal journey with which you have now chosen to experience in this physical form.

You have been, and always will be, on your path to purpose in this lifetime, whether you are conscious of it yet or not. You are here as a willing participant of the global consciousness that is creating our human reality, and part of your purpose is to simply contribute your energy by interacting in the world!

Beyond that, you also have more specific purpose gifts to discover and deliver which, in addition to helping others, will bring joy and deep meaning to your life. You are a powerfully creative being. Digging deeper is the way to create your dreams, and dream your way to creating your destiny. The further you explore your own ability to create from your deepest desires, the further you will be able to go on your limitless lifetime journey.

"Life is short and every day is precious: Expect the good!"

Your life is a *precious gift* that has been given to you, and you are a precious gift to others as you live and give like the G.E.M. that you are. You have already been living your purpose by helping yourself and others, creating a lot of good and making a big difference in the lives you touch with your loving energy. When you give yourself credit for *being* and doing the good, you will be energized with the emotional thoughts to expect more of the good.

It's important to take a moment to reflect on where you have already been on your journey to understand that you were born creating your own life of purpose. The key to learning how to create a more joyful life is to look back at when you have been joyful and connect the dots. Hopefully, you have had much joy, laughed a lot, and have had moments of total bliss that were unforgettable. No doubt, they were all moments when you felt loved, lovable, playful, and light.

In those times, you were also sharing your joy, laughter, humor, and lightness with others in a way that you were uplifting each other reciprocally. That is one of the most important ways to help others; being joyful, light, and uplifting to enhance your life and the lives of others who are with you. Making life more fun (good) for others is a powerful way of making life much better (good) for you too.

Your purpose is also about exploration and growth; learning from both the ups and downs of your experience. If you look back on your life, there will be some memories of events that will obviously reflect your growth when you compare it to your current point of perspective. The memories may now make you cringe with regret, giggle with delight at what you got away with, or remember that you were just naïve.

You could conclude that, back then, you didn't know any better and now, you have more life experience and clarity about what you are doing. If only you knew then what you know now, you wouldn't have done what you did.

Well, what if you did *know*? Most likely, it's true that you knew better and with rebellious or juvenile intentions, you did it anyway! Or, perhaps you knew that you had to do it, without fully realizing it, to somehow show yourself something new and different in order to grow or to expand yourself. Surely, you already know that you are here to create your life and learn from it. You see that even the bad stuff you go through can be good for you if it brings about personal growth.

You are naturally led by your inner desire, curiosity, and drive to explore life, and you learn more, or grow the most, by living it rather than reading or hearing about it. Somewhere inside, even when you were very young, there was an inner voice that led you to make each choice that you have made. Your inner self has always been teaching you about life and is still influencing what you do. So, now what will you do? You will automatically do what you already have been doing, until you desire to seek more clarity and dig even deeper.

"Your own being creates your own doing: Own your power."

When you own what you've known, you'll be shown when you've grown. As you begin to own your power, you will be awakening your inner guidance by learning how to ask questions and listen for the answers that emerge from within. By asking the right questions or the best questions for clarity, you will bring forth the insightful answers that you will receive and the better results that will occur from applying them into action.

Simply put, apply what you know and the benefits will show. Your ability to *listen* to your inner answers will develop with time after you fully

embrace that your inner guidance is real because the insights are prov-
ing to be consistently accurate and helpful. Absolute clarity, then, comes
from the realization that you do own your power of being and do know
the answers to your questions.

That inner power, along with the clarity that comes with it, is what
enables you to enhance your life with the awareness of purpose. Your
purpose path continually evolves with your personal growth and, as
you will discover, your purpose involves much more than what you are
doing day to day or what you do for a living.

You can know that you are already on your purpose path when you accept that your life purpose does not derive from what you are doing or
fail because you are not yet doing it. Rather, your purpose is primarily
brought about by your state of *being* or who you are energetically being,
how you are expressing yourself, when and why you are acting out your
intentions, and what energy you are giving to yourself and others.

Without getting into the details about Universal Laws, such as The
Law of Attraction, your energy is given out and received by others, and
you will get back a vibrational match in return. Just as gravity is always
in play, whether you see it or not, in the same way, this energy exchange
is happening in every moment of your life journey. Having the *conscious
awareness* that your being is in play just like that, in time, will show you
evidence of this truth.

By focusing on how your energy of being is affecting yourself and others, you can observe it over and over again until you have undoubtedly
proven it to yourself. That is, you will see that the way in which you
are showing up for others is being reflected back by the way others are
showing up for you. Then, you will know that you do own your power
to create your desired life experience.

"Your natural state is joy: Joy raises your attraction frequency."

When you raise your *vibrational frequency* to a state of positive being, your vibrational matches will return to you in the form of positive experiences that resonate at the same energy frequency. Your energy of being is directly related to your emotional thoughts, words, behaviors, and actions. Your vibrational energy matters greatly as you shape your own life and impact the lives of others with your current state of being.

Like an energetic Ping-Pong match, you set up your future experiences with your present state of being—the positive attracting positive, and the negative attracting negative. So, when you work to allow your being to habitually vibrate with higher states of joy, love, and positivity, you will reap the higher rewards that will make this self-discovery process worth the effort. Finding your joy and sharing it will help you and those you help to live the best version of the future.

You have been designed to be and to create the energy of love, and your natural state is joy itself. Your *grand design* has equipped you with everything you need to manifest your desires (truth), bring forth your personal message (love), deliver your gifts (joy), and live an impactful life of joyous purpose (freedom). By allowing yourself to embrace this as your truth of authentic expression, as who you are being, you will be living an exhilarating life of joy as higher vibration. As you bring this into your living experience, you will enjoy more inner peace and a greater sense of freedom from despair and self-doubt.

Joy has always been available to you and a part of your life experience whether or not you have been noticing it or focusing upon it. Developing the habit of noticing your joy (of the past, the present, and the future) will illuminate the evidence that you always live on your joyous path to purpose. The inner voice of positive light is the real messenger of truth, love, joy, and freedom, living inside of you as your authentic inner guide or inner knowing.

That is the positive *soul voice* to listen for when you are asking for answers, as it sounds grounded, balanced, reassuring, and optimistic. It will encourage you and awaken your authentic truth that guides you to higher perceptions, greater understanding, and deeper purpose. It always sends messages as kind, love-based, compassionate insights which create calmness, gratitude, and empowering beliefs that bring about the greater good for all.

"Fear is illusion that causes confusion: Listen to your soul voice!"

Just as inner guidance is, and always will be, part of you in life, so is inner resistance. Joyfulness lights up your path with positive purpose as inner guidance, and fearfulness darkens your path with negative suffering, as inner resistance. While fear can protect one from real danger, it also blocks joy or the enlightenment that occurs as a deeper connection with inner knowing, positivity, and love.

At the very worst, fear is a serious distraction, an illusion, a convincing false truth, where the inner *saboteur voice* thrives. Your negative saboteur voice continually breeds fear-based beliefs and lies that emerge from the wounded, darker side of the *ego*, causing inner suffering, discouraging you from owning your power, or believing in your higher purpose. It brings deception, manipulation, and distrust into your experience and promotes a need for control, a lack of empathy, selfishness, and greed.

Fear can also show up as self-doubt: anger, disappointment, guilt, shame, blame, worry, and irrational feelings of insecurity that can influence you against using or believing in your personal gifts. Even though you are not deficient, broken, or without gifts to contribute, these habitual negative perceptions can condition you, convince you otherwise, and get stored in the subconscious mind as self-criticism or self-loathing.

It is possible to heal negative inner wounding by practicing positive affirmations or positive self-talk and silencing the fearful inner dialog. To keep it simple, you can learn to conquer fear with love, confusion with truth, anger with joy, and resistance with freedom; releasing emotional pain by letting go with forgiveness, acceptance, tolerance, empathy, responsibility and kindness. Your soul voice of positivity will be there when you are in various states of fear, so remember to listen to your soul self-talk of hope and positive born-wisdom instead of the lies of the self-destructive saboteur.

Learning this, too, is a part of your purpose journey that will bring you back, full-circle, to joy. Recognizing how to find joy in the moment will remind you that you are right where you are supposed to be—on your joyous path to purpose.

"Everything makes energy, and everything takes energy: Give love and joy!"

Now that you know where you are, you can see that the energy you make takes your energy, and the energy you take-in also makes more energy. Focusing on being the good energy will allow you to be in your heart and able to give more love and joy, which is the main point of *purpose living*. To be in your heart means that you are energetically feeling, speaking, listening, responding, and creating with loving intention. This requires the ability to express or communicate your honest truth to others, as your authentic self, with emotionally intelligent compassion, empathy, gratitude, and kind understanding. It takes energy to be this joyful version of yourself, and it makes a big difference in what you can create for yourself and for those around you.

Having this emotional intelligence is a *developed ability*, an acquired skill, which utilizes your heart-brain connection to create the focus and presence of love and joy. It happens in the moment, in the joy of now, and you can tap into that loving energy at any time, any place, anywhere. Giving others your love and joy comes from being present for them as you listen and respond with positivity. Being uplifting energy helps them to see their own self-worth and align with optimism which will, in turn, raise their frequency.

As you now understand, purpose living comes out of knowing your own self-worth and embracing the truth that your life matters to all that you help with your energy. Your energy, as your state of being, greatly affects what you are doing and the way in which your perceptions and actions play out to help yourself, others, and the world. When you are being a G.E.M. in the world, you are creating another G.E.M. with your energy; and when it multiplies to infinity, we are *one consciousness* together.

Your conscious awakening is the process of developing a deeper connection with your inner born-wisdom, your truth, and your own self-love. You are a real G.E.M., and knowing yourself means knowing your priceless and precious value that only you can deliver in this lifetime. It's time to dig deep by asking yourself daily questions, praying, meditating, and listening for your soul voice answers as you journal your progress. Silence yourself and listen closely; pay attention to the messages of your emotional thoughts, your dreams, and your intuitive feelings of what life is showing you every day. With practice, you will have the clarity to envision and create your happiest life.

Creating a *positive environment* is crucial to being able to continually progress, learn to your fullest potential, and contribute your personal life-purpose gifts. In youth, you developed as a product of your environment. As an adult, you are setting the stage, influencing your environment with what you are accumulatively learning as your life journey unfolds. With continued awareness of this, you will progress faster and further than you could have previously imagined. It is possible to be living the best life of your dreams as you keep aiming for higher vibrations.

This journey is never complete; you are always guided, creating and influencing your experiences by interacting with your *eternal energy*. You are destined to give and receive love and joy freely from your heart space, and while enduring the ups and downs and the distractions of life, you are love and joy. You are on your Joyous Path to Purpose!

———•·•◦•·•———

Bonnie Gordon Patterino has been a Life Transformation Leader for over thirty years. After graduating from Penn State in 1985, her health and wellness career blossomed from being Assistant Director at The White House Athletic Center to owning Vows & Wows Wellness Spa. Her creative coaching methods have helped thousands of people to "transform from the inside out". Now, beyond nurturing and pampering her Spa clients with beauty treatments, she offers expanded ways of developing spiritual, emotional, physical, and mental well-being from within.

She empathically recognizes that most people need to become aware of their life purpose gifts, fueling themselves with those new motivations, to build vitality and a zest for life. Bonnie's personal self-discovery and self-healing journey, combined with her continued education and career experience, has contributed to her innovative coaching abilities that lead to one's self-actualization. Her life purpose gifts have led her to help herself while developing a plan, a message and a method that empowers others to heal inner pain and defeat paralyzing obstacles. She understands that people often underestimate themselves because they are conditioned by negative beliefs. Her message emphasizes how to face and conquer fears, and find personal empowerment through love and joyful contribution.

Her targeted life mission is to globally help others embrace self-worth and self-love through her original Guidance Power System™. This

GPS system utilizes her Energy Life Maps Coaching™ for clarity and life balance, and Energy Alignment Therapies™ for emotional release and self-healing. She combines cognitive processes, vibrational energy healing techniques, and meditative states to reveal inner answers and create inner harmony. After having success with individuals, groups and audiences, her ultimate dream is to deliver her GPS system, **GPS Your Path**™ method, as a life training tool for holistic practitioners, life coaches and therapists who would spread this help world-wide.

Bonnie, Owner of Vows & Wows, Inc. and GPS Your Path™, can be contacted at gpsyourpath@gmail.com, 301-428-7288 or www.gpsyourpath.com.

Be Authentically You

Authentic Self vs. Practiced Self

Cynthia Stott

Our Authentic Self can be very different than our Practiced Self. This doesn't mean that there is something *wrong* with you in your current stage of "Practiced vs. Authentic Self." In fact, you are in your most perfect and best "self" right here and now, and the more you can accept and appreciate this truth, the more authentic you will become.

The trick or conundrum with the Practiced Self vs. Authentic Self is that as you become more and more authentic, you might feel uncomfortable or even have thoughts and feelings of *"this is not me"* because our Authentic Selves are truly unstoppable and can feel and appear very different than our Practiced Selves.

Let me explain what I mean by Practiced Self. It is the self that we have been and became over the years, mostly coming from beliefs and experiences that we had in our childhood and youth. In fact, most of our beliefs (unless we have worked to change or *rewire* them in a subconscious way) come from our babyhood and childhood. Many psychologists believe that the majority of our beliefs and mindset were *set* by the time we were 12 years old.

Let me explain further with an example of my own Practiced Self. I lived for nearly 40 years with tremendous fear. I had four strong phobias—speaking, dancing, spiders, and heights—and many, many other fears that could be considered phobias. I was the most fearful person I knew personally, and even one of my best friends called me a "wuss." (Okay, we met in the '80s and the polite definition of this word was an overly fearful person.) She wasn't being mean; she was just being truthful.

Like many Light Workers, I grew up in a very challenging environment. I wasn't only different; I lived in a very violent and actually danger-ous and abusive environment. Consequently, parts of me broke off and formed strong ego parts to protect me and help me survive the "war zone" that I grew up in. Then as an adult, these parts continued to do their "job" even though I no longer lived in that physically dangerous environment. I guess it was a form of Post-Traumatic Stress Disorder (PTSD), like soldiers often get in combat situations, that left me de-bilitated in many ways. I wouldn't open a dictionary or encyclopedia because I was afraid that I might touch a picture of a spider, and I hugged the wall in the Seattle Space Needle because I was too afraid to even approach the window. I was no longer in real danger, but because of my past, they certainly felt real to me.

After going on a spiritual and self-development journey where I ex-perimented with many modalities and methods to overcome fear, these fears have nearly disappeared for me. In fact, most people who know me now can't believe that I was ever that fearful and think I must be exaggerating because they no longer see, feel, or recognize this type of fear in me. I still have fear at times. I think this is just part of being human, but they are much *bigger* fears that often have real danger as-sociated with them. Regarding my four strong phobias—I speak for a living; dance with abandon and freedom (even on stage); think small spiders are *cute*; and did a 17-story bungee jump and loved it! My whole attitude and relationship with fear has changed.

Strangely, and this is where the *"that's not me"* part of experiencing my Practiced Self vs. Authentic Self comes in for me, is that now things that could be dangerous often don't scare me. When I was going on a kayaking trip in Hawaii, the instructor asked if any of us were afraid or concerned about sharks. My immediate *gut* reaction was a verbal and confident, *"NO."* This response shocked me and I thought, *"Who said that?"* One of the others in the group piped up and said, "Well I am," although a bit sheepishly. It was my Authentic Self that said "no" so confidently. The truth was that I didn't feel any fear about possible sharks in that moment because I was developing a new Practiced Self that was closer and in more alignment with my Authentic Self. However, my old Practiced Self was a bit puzzled by this turn of events.

Often the obstacles that we face or wounds we develop in our Practiced Selves become our greatest strengths and gifts when we live from our Authentic Selves. My overly fearful Practiced Self, who didn't feel safe even when there was no real danger, has become a sort of "safety professional" or "overcoming fear expert" as I am stepping more and more into my Authentic Self. Now I provide the entrepreneurs and speakers I serve with tools and processes to overcome fears and inner-obstacles so you can become more and more of your Authentic Self and serve the people you are meant to serve with your greatest and unique gifts.

The truth of the matter is your Authentic Self is truly unstoppable. It is also true that all of you—the things you might now consider good, bad, ugly, and beautiful—all of it is actually good and beautiful and can be used by you as you step deeper and deeper—and yes, greater and greater—into being your most Authentic Self.

The truth is, you are perfect and complete, right here, right now; and you are unstoppable, beautiful, and eternal. This is who you truly are.

There is a formula that I have discovered—CPA. A CPA is an expert, and this is an expert of a different sort, an expert formula that can lead you deeper into becoming your Authentic Self.

CPA, Three Steps to Authenticity

Curiosity: How does curiosity lead to authenticity? When we get curious, magic happens! Curiosity is a wonderful and powerful thing and can lead us deeper into our Authentic Selves, if we allow it.

Cindy Sue, my Inner-Wisdom Child (an aspect of my Higher Self), is a playful and wise child within me that is always encouraging me to be more and more curious about everything—the good, the bad, the ugly, the beautiful, the challenges and the blessings in my life.

Getting curious and asking questions—not *accusatory* questions, but real curious questions—is a powerful way to transform or transmute negative emotions, thought, and fears. Shining the light of curiosity can transform our fears, like shining a flashlight under the bed of a child can show him/her that there is no "Boogeyman" under the bed, only toys and dust bunnies. Shining the light of curiosity on our fears takes away their power.

Best of all, curiosity can be a guide to go deeper into your Authentic Self by helping you discover more and more about your passions—the next step in the CPA formula.

Passion: "I am Passionate about Passion!" I have come to understand that much like curiosity, passion can change everything. In fact, passion sells! Our passion and enthusiasm is a great "Enroller" to our cause and what most matters to us. It is the "secret ingredient" to any sales conversation, whether it be with your spouse or partner about having dinner out vs. cooking-in; 2-year-olds on brushing their teeth or eating their peas; or a $20-million business deal. Passion is a powerful tool!

Our passions—those things that make our hearts sing—are powerful keys to whom your Authentic Self truly is. In fact, following, discovering, and honoring your passions is one of the greatest self-discovery and spiritual journeys you can embark upon.

Many of us (myself included) have a hard time identifying, recognizing, and especially honoring our greatest passions by ourselves. We often need the "mirror" of another person—a trusted friend, loved one, coach, mentor, or even an "enemy"—to help us see our deepest passions and our greatest gifts. Many times we might say, *"Oh no, that can't be it… that's too easy…anyone can do that…"* Because these passions and gifts are so close to us—so much a part of us—we just can't see them or appreciate and honor them like others can.

Here's an experiment: Try to see the nose on your face without a mirror. We usually can't see our own nose, without wrinkling up our face in some unnatural way, without the outside perspective of a mirror. In a similar way, we can't see—and especially honor and appreciate—our passions and gifts because we are too close to them. We need the space and reflection of a mirror to properly see them.

Another outside perspective is the perspective of our heart, soul, Higher Self or even God, universe, inner-knowing—whatever you call that part of you that has a broader, deeper perspective and may even know everything about you. You can ask that part of yourself for a new, deeper perspective on your deepest passions and gifts with this simple prayer or meditation. (I have heard it said that prayer is talking to God and meditation is listening to the answers.) In this exercise, we do both the talking/asking and most of all the listening.

Passions and Gifts Meditation

Sit quietly with your feet on the floor or in any comfortable seated position.

Place your hands on your heart center in the center of your chest, gently and easily.

Breathe in and out—with a sigh, completely letting go of all stress and tension.

Breathe in and out—letting more and more tension leave your body with your audible sigh.

Breathe in and out—completely relaxing and letting go of any tension.

Take at least three of these deep relaxing breaths until you feel relaxed, centered, and supported by the ease of your breath.

With your hands on your heart, feel your heart.

With closed eyes, smile at your heart.

Ask your heart, "What am I most passionate about? What makes my heart sing?"

Listen for its response—in words, pictures, feelings, memories—however your heart wants to communicate with you.

If nothing comes to you, don't worry (this is natural)—just breathe in and out again and then ask, "What am I most passionate about? What makes my heart sing?"

Listen. Patiently and lovingly listen.

Repeat until you get a response—no matter how small or inconsequential it may seem (these can actually be our greatest gifts, like the still, small voice inside of us).

When you're ready (or even at another time), you can ask more questions —get curious; like, "I am listening. Please tell me more about this passion or gift." Or, "I don't understand, please show me more and help me to understand about this passion or gift."

Be honest. Be honest with your heart and tell it you don't understand; you're confused; or you're even afraid of this passion or gift. Your heart already knows your thoughts and the more honest, vulnerable, and authentic you can be with your heart, the more trust you will build with it.

The good news is that you don't have to take immediate action on what your heart shows you as your greatest passions and gifts. You are just exploring right now, getting more and more curious.

Once you have a better idea and understanding of your passions and gifts and have shared any fears or doubts with your heart about it and sought your heart's guidance, you can ask deeper and more practical questions.

- *"What are some easy, practical steps that I can take in the next days or weeks to develop and reconnect with these passions and gifts?"*
- *"Who needs me to share these passions and gifts with them?"*
- *"How can I find the people that need these passions and gifts most?"*
- *"Who can support me in these passions and gifts?"*
- *"Who can help me bring my passions and gifts to the people I can serve best with them?"*

These questions are literally endless. You can ask as many questions as you like, just make sure to pause, breathe, and listen for and to the answers.

When you are finished, thank your heart for sharing its wisdom.

Breathe in and out.

Breathe in and out.

Breathe in and out.

Slowly open your eyes and look around the room for any green color, or any other color, that will bring you back to the here and now.

How do you feel? I hope you feel wonderful! However you feel—relaxed, excited, warm or cold, happy, or touched emotionally—it is perfect, exactly what you needed. You can't do this exercise wrong and every time you do it, you may get different answers and/or feelings. Just keep asking and listening.

This leads us to our next step...acceptance.

Acceptance: We are wonderful and perfect in all our imperfections. The more you accept this as truth and have compassion with yourself, the more you will become your most Authentic Self.

The final key in this journey of becoming your most Authentic Self is acceptance. It is a journey and, fortunately, you will never reach a static, solid Authentic Self because the more you journey into your Authentic Self, the more layers and richness you will uncover and discover.

It's like a life-long soul mate journey where you just keep loving the other person and finding more and more things that you love about them. Just like a soul mate journey, every day is not full of "roses and butterflies"—it is a cyclical and ever-changing journey where you have to show your commitment and dedication to honoring your relationship. You have to be willing to forgive and have compassion with yourself just like a relationship with another loved one. In essence, you have to become your own beloved. The interesting thing is, the more beloved you become to yourself, the more others will become beloved to you and you to them.

Love always multiplies; it never divides. You will find your love is endless, just like the power of your unstoppable Authentic Self.

So what will this message mean to you? Are you ready to get curious and courageous and find out who you really are? It's simple, but not easy. *"Who Am I? What do I really want? What am I most Passionate about?"* These are some of the most powerful questions we can ask ourselves. It takes courage and vulnerability to ask and then listen for and to the answers. You may have many doubts and fears that come up as you ask these questions. In fact, your heart may say things like, *"You don't really want to know, do you?"* or *"Why do you want to do this now? We have plenty of time to answer these questions later."* Or your To-Do list might start calling to you.

Let me share with you a journey where my heart/soul/Higher Self put up some roadblocks and obstacles to these questions and how that HELPED me to become more committed and determined to find out the answers.

Journey to Meet my Soul: A Story of Curiosity, Passion, and Acceptance

It's interesting that when we are told that we can't have or do something, we tend to want it even more. This phenomenon is as old as Adam and Eve and the "Forbidden Fruit." Usually we identify the "tempter" of this forbidden thing as the Devil—many times this "tempter" is actually our

Higher Self, soul, an angel or even God. Like when Jacob wrestled with the angels, sometimes we need a wrestling match to prepare ourselves to receive the highest and best information.

I was given the opportunity to attend a very special training in Sedona, Arizona, among the powerful energy vortexes. In this training, I was going to meet my soul face-to-face, as it were. I was so excited! Then I heard that I would come back with a new name—*"WHAT? But I like my name! Why would I want a new name?"*

"This is your soul's name," I heard my yoga master say, *"And we will call you by it going forward."*

I really wanted to meet my soul, but I wasn't comfortable with changing my name.

I went to the training, and it was the most powerful training I have ever experienced. Meeting my soul felt pretty simple, straight-forward, easy, and extremely lovely and powerful. It was in a swimming pool—so natural for me as I LOVE swimming! When I met my soul, it was like a great flash of light that filled the pool, and my soul sparkled and shined like a many-pointed Christmas tree star, only much bigger. This meeting was so profound and beautiful, but it left many questions afterward as it was only a glimpse of my soul. I wanted to know more.

The next day I found out that we were going to have the opportunity to ask our soul its name and then go through a naming ceremony where we would take on our soul's name. Oh, this time taking on another name didn't sound so bad, and I was really curious and wanted to know my soul's name. I was actually excited to know its name! Still not so sure about changing my name, but wanted to know its name.

I was a bit nervous, but mostly excited when it came time to find out my soul's name. I followed the instructions, but something strange began to happen—my soul started teasing me! It said things like, "You can make-up a name; no one will know."

I said, *"I don't want to make-up a name; I want to know your name. Tell me your name."*

After hemming and hawing, it finally said, *"Ma—yeah, you can do something with that."*

"What do you mean 'I can do something with that—I want to know YOUR NAME, not some made-up name. Tell me YOUR NAME."

We went back and forth like this for several minutes. I could hear people stirring and knew that they had already gotten their souls' names. I was beginning to get nervous that I wouldn't get my name and felt bad that I might be holding the others up from the naming ceremony because they had already gotten their names. My soul just wasn't being very cooperative!

So I started to argue with my soul, and my impatience and frustration kept building until I got down right demanding! I think I even started to use my physical hands while talking with my soul and even made fists at one point. Then with the energy of grabbing my soul by its collar or the scruff of its neck I DEMANDED, *"TELL ME YOUR NAME!!!"*

Then I heard it. Chun Ji Ma Um. It was in Korean. (I was in a Korean yoga practice.) But, I knew these words: Chun (Heaven); Ji (Earth); Ma Um (Heart-Mind) is the literal translation. It means Cosmic Consciousness or in other words, "The Mind that Thought the Original Thought that Created Everything."

This was a very BIG NAME and it scared me! Immediately, I started arguing again—only this time with a much more reverent tone as I was now humbled by this NAME and recognized who I was dealing with. I said to my soul in a rather sheepish and scholarly way, "I don't know the rules, but I'm pretty sure that I can't take THAT name."

My soul patiently repeated, *"Chun Ji Ma Um."*

"But I can't take that NAME. I'm sure it would be against the rules," I said with sort of a pleading voice, now feeling extremely humble and even insignificant as I faced the vastness and power of my SOUL.

I continued to plead and resist taking this name as my soul's voice got louder and louder and more and more commanding—*"Chung Ji Ma Um! CHUN JI MA UM!"* Until it got so LOUD, BOOMING and actually DEMANDED—*"CHUN JI MA UM!"*

I started to cry. I felt so humble and even afraid—afraid to the depth of my being—afraid I would violate some Cosmic Law or something. Remember that uncomfortable feeling that we talked about earlier—the one we can get when we step deeper into our Authentic Selves—it went way past uncomfortable and into fear and trepidation! At the same time, I realized that I was being given an opportunity and a gift. If I didn't accept this gift, the opportunity might be lost forever.

With gratitude, humbleness, and responsibility, I finally agreed to accept my NAME. With tears streaming down my face I said, *"Yes. I accept. I accept this NAME. I Am Chun Ji Ma Um."*

This was a very BIG NAME. I didn't know and couldn't even imagine what it would mean to accept this NAME, and I knew that my life would be different from this moment on. I was willing (and even a little bit excited) to see what would happen.

When I walked on stage to officially accept my soul's name with the Naming Ceremony, I paused to ask the officiating Yoga Master the burning question that was on my mind. *"I don't know the rules. Am I allowed to take this NAME?"*

He laughed and said, *"Yes, of course! It's a Good Name; it's a Great Name! It's a BIG NAME, and you are allowed to take it."*

Whew! I was so relieved! I guess I wasn't violating some Cosmic Law by accepting this NAME, after all. I relaxed and with gratitude, humbleness, and responsibility I took on the name Chun Ji Ma Um. I was called by this name by everyone in my yoga community until I left that community four years later. It was very uncomfortable at the beginning, especially because I needed to explain its meaning to all the English-speaking members. I think it was even more difficult to experience the reaction of the Korean members. They would pause, re-read my name tag, gasp, and then ask me, *"Do you know what name means?"* In the beginning I would say, *"Yes,"* with a humble smile and blush. They would usually explain it to me anyway—in their version of what the name meant to them. This was very enlightening as it seemed so personal to each and every one of them, as if they were describing their own grandmother or someone very dear and precious to them.

As I got more and more comfortable with the name and stepping deeper into my Authentic Self, my *"Yes"* got more comfortable and confident, and I started giving it with a knowing smile. Then they would usually drop the description, give me a good "look-over," look deep into my eyes; then, give a smile and a nod of the head. Once I shared it with a Korean woman outside of the community whom I had just met—this was a big risk for me! She did a comprehensive "look-over" of me—with a little bit of *"could this be true?"* energy—then peered deep into my eyes and concluded, *"Yes, You Are!"*

Up until this point, I have shared this story with people (outside my yoga community) only in private. The Korean stranger I shared it with was pretty "safe" as we were in Dallas, Texas, (far from my home in San Francisco at the time), and she was from New Zealand. This writing is the first time I have ever shared this deeply personal and authentic story publically.

Who we truly are is so BIG, POWERFUL, and UNSTOPPABLE! I believe the truth is that, at our highest and deepest selves, we are ALL Cosmic Consciousness, God, Source, Creator, whatever you call it. We are like drops in the ocean and together we form the vast ocean that is our universe. We ebb and flow, tumble and fall—all a part of the Great Spirit of the Ocean that is LIFE.

Get curious. Go deeper into your journey to find your essence in your passions and with passion. Accept more and more the power of who you are. Be Authentically YOU!

———————

Cynthia Stott is a Speaker Mentor and Success Mindset Expert. She is Passionate about Passion and helping you get paid well for doing what you LOVE. She believes when you show up in the world authentically, whether on stage or in ordinary life, magic happens. Her signature belief changing system has been called the "Holy Grail" and helps to release the emotional charge from past traumatic events so you can be more of your authentic self and shine your Light in the world more effortlessly.

Mission-Driven Entrepreneurs and Speakers work with Cynthia to develop their Inner Business Power so they can get PAID WELL for doing what they LOVE! For more information about her business The Speakers Summit™ or Cynthia go to www.CynthiaStott.com

Becoming Sovereign: A Journey Into Consciousness

Lynda Bradley, M.A.

If we only had a brief time together, what would I most like to share with you about my quest—this quest to find comforting answers to the mysteries of my own life. For me, the words "Becoming Sovereign" are the same as describing "Whole, Perfect, and Complete." Because when we are all these three—like the title of this book— we are boundless, independent, self-reliant, and absolute! We are the rulers over ourselves, and most importantly, we become Masters of our Consciousness.

Inspiration

Are you able to believe naturally and automatically that you are complete? Or would you sometimes need to understand and be reminded that it is true, and why it is true, and how to arrive there?

We must witness our worth for ourselves. All our external supports will not be sufficient to ensure that we feel truly self-reliant. We must actually experience the sunlight shining, not only down on us, but inside us, and know that wherever this light resides, darkness cannot co-exist.

If we are discouraged, clichéd concepts do not comfort us. We become numb to inspiration and lose touch with our source energy. But by developing our consciousness along with its component aspects of purpose, intuition, meditation, and intention, we are then better able to reconnect to feeling whole, perfect, and complete.

We seek answers constantly to questions about our life, health, career, and relationships. And usually we search among mentors and specialists in the external world or occasionally among intuitive counselors. But most often, we do not look to our greatest resource—ourselves. You, when "Sovereign," will always reside deep in your center, rather than at the periphery of yourself. In addition, you will carry this completeness wherever you go, without needing to feel at the center of groups.

Who are you that no one else can be?

Each of us is absolutely unique. We may have similar identities, but they are never identical. We each have a valuable contribution that no other person would be able to replicate exactly in the same manner. To find this uniqueness, to embrace it and develop it, is so critically important for stability, success, and happiness.

Throughout years of facilitating Meditation Trainings, I gave an assignment to determine "what would sustain you when all else vanishes." Students spoke about family, friends, or material possessions, yet no one had understood this critical question—that the search must proceed through the gates within, solely towards our inner selves—a quest that is aimed toward Mastership and Sovereignty.

Following a lifetime of Metaphysical Studies with sages and mystics, my own identity has crystallized now as an Intuitive Energy Specialist. My hope in this book is to simplify life concepts and infuse them with practical meaning. Throughout these pages, I describe classic yet simple techniques for you to become self-reliant and "Sovereign."

Purpose

Where do we start?

"KNOW THYSELF" has been one of the most pivotal philosophies through the ages. This concept from ancient Egypt and Greece has been connected with the great teachers Hermes, Thoth, and Socrates.

Why is this purpose so very important? It is so because every moment that you exist without yourself as your prime mentor, your trusted counselor, and your internal commander—every moment without this critical guidance is so much more difficult than it ever need be.

During these disconnected periods, we relinquish access to our intuition for perceptions, decisions, healings, and empowerment. Dedicated voyages into our consciousness are needed to showcase our core identities and abbreviate life challenges. It can be extremely inconvenient not to know the ways of the world, but it can be devastating not to know oneself.

My work in the field of Hospice Care was deeply pivotal for me. I witnessed many patients nearing their final hours without meaningful preparation, despite a lifetime of opportunities. They had always hidden among worldly activities, never creating a haven of solace within and, therefore, remained strangers to themselves as they approached their transition.

In our global societies, the failure to "know thyself" and to regulate responses to situations is too often followed by catastrophic effects. Throughout history, there exist too many examples of individuals unable to determine rational or intuitive solutions within the personal, social, political, legal, and ethical arenas.

Consciousness

"Consciousness" is one of those words often used incorrectly. It is perhaps the most important energy both inside of us and outside of us—a force of energetic intelligence, without boundaries. It extends far beyond the internal technology of the mind-brain system, and also far beyond the external technology of machine constructs.

At birth or before, our consciousness is intended to be the first human activation and to remain so until we depart from our life journey.

This force of intelligent energy is the engine in our lives. It is both the pen and the story in our evolution. In this new millennium, consciousness becomes the final frontier for exploration, and we are its consequential stewards moving us toward higher octaves. The answers that we seek are already within us long before the questions have been formed.

Intuition

Intuition is a method of interpreting energy, and it is a necessary skill for self-reliance. When we refer to "energy," we mean the vibrations that reside in all objects, animate and inanimate. Intuition contributes to our wisdom, as it involves the science of assessing and classifying all energies, visible and invisible, sensory and extra-sensory. The skill of intuition requires a continuous hyper-awareness combined with a precise discrimination. In order to *"go with the flow"* we must first be able to sense the flow, proceeding beyond linear logic.

Throughout the years, my own path of exploration has been mainly scientific. However, as a result of intense meditation combined with extensive clinical work, I became acutely intuitive, eventually receiving information from what would be called my Higher Self.

To develop intuition, our observation skills in the visible world can be honed and then replicated in the non-visible areas. For example, we may practice awareness using metrics such as quantity, location, temperature, and qualities. In assessing visible energy, we observe that a blizzard produces snow which is in excess, in the exterior, piled high, very cold, falling fast. But these same metrics may be transferred to more subtle areas. A human personality can be reported intuitively as deficient, internally cold, passive, and slow.

As we move toward Sovereignty, we must also become Masters of Energy. We need the ability to recognize and to control varied states of consciousness. Each will have its identifying emotional/mental matrix. We must also be adept at creating and reversing these states "on command"—for example, shifting between: courage and caution; consistency and flexibility; cooperation and control.

Meditation

Meditation enhances the flow and balance of energy. The practice of any method of meditation can be a valuable key to our consciousness. It is a vehicle to locating our source energy, our Higher Self, and ultimately to becoming Sovereign.

Why meditate? Quite simply, because it will lead you back "Home" and launch you into a process of self-discovery. It exposes us to the truth of our own essence and also to a larger tapestry of Life. Well apart from documented health benefits, meditation can generate your most enlightened decisions. It augments a myopic vision beyond the consensus reality. Throughout the many disciplines I have embraced, meditation has proven to be the most valuable of all.

Meditation: Portable and Fast

During my journeys, I designed a most effective method of meditation which is portable and fast.

Unlike the traditional sedentary system, this one is completely portable. It may occur with eyes wide open or in a group or with noise... moments stolen during a normal day, while stopping at a traffic light, washing hands, entering an elevator, waiting in line, doing mundane tasks, or from a more radical perspective, while listening to others converse! Even in a very public setting, when I distance myself internally from the outside environment, dividing my awareness into at least two areas, I feel an increasing sense of "me." Being able to isolate our true selves in a tornado of chaotic energies is extremely valuable.

When practical, I recall my techniques using "S" words: stop, separate, seek silence, survey in secure space. During this process, I become aware of self and from this center, this control tower, I objectively evaluate all energies with clarity. Within this silence, my issues distill to their essential core and healing solutions surface. This deep inner comprehension produces an outer calm, as strength builds from within.

Once located, our inner world is so personal that it becomes a sacred space. It offers complete privacy for us to rejuvenate. Most importantly, amid this sacred energy, we find the insights to become Sovereign.

However, we rarely have sufficient time in our 21st century world to meditate in a formal manner. So, in addition to being portable, this type of meditation is fast. The skill to withdraw wherever we find ourselves becomes imperative then—in a crowded place, eyes wide open, hearing ambient noises, separating our consciousness into a duality, at minimum, or even more segments. We are able to capture precious moments from our day by separating "on command" from our environment.

For many years I was a practitioner in the field of Complementary Medicine. I had only moments to shift, to empty out, and to recalibrate between patients, focusing at the door between rooms, releasing many details of energies, diagnoses, personalities. Maximizing each opportunity, even the smallest one, must be the objective for reconnecting and "knowing thyself."

Meditation: Prayer, & Visualization

Meditation can be a very different exercise than that of prayer. Prayer takes the form of insistent asking for specific answers, often with a busy mind. Contrary to this, in meditation, we await and maintain silence, listening in this void for understandings that appear spontaneously. It can be said that while prayer involves active asking, meditation requires more passive listening.

The technique of visualization, however, may be used during either prayer or meditation. Energetically it is an "active" technique where we use our consciousness to mentally "paint a picture." And then as we combine our emotions with these visualized pictures, this process forms the basis for intention.

Intention

Intention involves a deliberate resolve, which sends our energy to a specific target. It channels the force of our will and acts as a compass on our path. When we visualize particular outcomes, by combining emotions with mental pictures, we become the artists and architects for our life.

For intention to be genuinely successful, three aspects, all applied with great precision, are required:

First, we need to clearly identify our desires before directing our will toward their manifestation.

Secondly, efforts made without sufficient intensity of emotions will not precipitate adequate results. In addition, the purity of emotion is a factor in choreographing the desired outcome. Any upgrade from a negative to a positive emotion improves our final product. The eventual goal would be the purist emotional vibration (joy, love). For example: anger is more effective than depression; doubt more positive than fear; belief stronger than hope.

Thirdly, and most important of all, this process is fastest when we assume that it is "already complete"—when the final product is felt to be crystallized here and now. Requests are not as effective if they are felt to be "in transit" or arriving in the future. In other words, our desires must be already present—arrived, complete, and manifest! For example, if we need sunshine to produce crops, we must feel now that warmth, taste now the meal, or see now the harvest reaped. We do not hope or expect, but rather we bask in its current reality. The predominant emotion is not anticipation, but instead, it is one of secure satisfaction.

A human life is composed of fractals and the law of intentionality can intercede to assemble them differently, changing and redirecting their patterns and consequences. From this quantum vantage point, everything then opens and shifts.

Your personal power resides firmly inside you and by using these techniques you may create a portal of precipitation for your desires. When we allow ourselves to imagine "what if?" then we ride on pure potential with a fearless enthusiasm that approaches magic. We are indeed the force itself, adapting to the tides of creation. This clarity of intention helps us to revisit our perfection.

Summary

In the quest within our spirit to become self-reliant and independent, we have examined five interwoven concepts. By committing to our inner development, these techniques will help us to attain mastery.

- Knowing yourself becomes your inspiring purpose.
- Consciousness is your engine for evolution.
- Intuition becomes your guiding wisdom.
- Meditation leads to your source energy.
- Intention directs the force of your will.

Every day decisions are made that affect our own lives and the lives of all those around us, extending throughout the entire planet. When we fail to connect with the intuitive wisdom deep inside our core, then we fail to see our path clearly. We risk ignoring our most vital energetic resource—that of our own personal energetic source.

A student asked me, *"What would the Buddha say about my Life?"*

I replied, *"I don't know what the Buddha would say, but after you have meditated—what would you yourself say about it?"*

YOU are The Force Manifest.

In closing, dear friends, I wish you wise journeys, using your consciousness for that stellar quest: Becoming a "Sovereign" Soul—Whole, Perfect, and Complete.

———•◦•◦•———

Lynda Bradley, M.A., is an Intuitive Bio-Energy Specialist. She has 20 years Clinical Experience licensed in Complementary Medicine, and 20 years of Spiritual Training in Meditation and Metaphysics. Lynda offers an advanced mode of Counseling, guiding individuals into rapid self-discovery, using Inner Gates as Portals into the Light. She assists clients in understanding their unique life-force patterns, enabling them to transcend obstacles and find their paths to clarity. For more details, please see: www.lyndabradley.com.

Personal Renaissance: A Revival Of Spirit

Laura Diana Lopez, M.A.

I see a picture in my mind's eye of a beautiful, joy-filled toddler, smiling ear-to-ear, with the light of the Universe still sparkling in her eyes. Her presence overwhelms me with love and compassion. I smile back at the vision of her and acknowledge that she has always been with me on this life's journey, tucked away deep within my heart. At times invisible even to my reflection in the mirror, at other times shining through my smile and my eyes for all the world to see. I bless her for choosing to live this life with me, for enduring all its challenges, and for introducing me to all the people I connected with because of the journey we chose.

Who is this radiant being, and how did her divine spark survive? When I remember myself at age three, what comes to mind is my mother tucking me in at night and telling me to *"be good"* for my dad, because she might not be there when I woke up. (I didn't know until years later what a difficult life my parents had as first-hand survivors of WWII, how anxiety and fear plagued them in their lives, and how much they longed for a fresh start.) I can now recognize that my mother was trying to give me a "heads up," but at the time all I felt was fear, as I tearfully

begged, *"Take me with you."* Her reply haunts me even now: *"Maybe…
If you're good."*

I lived through my childhood and teen years, never feeling good enough,
smart enough, thin enough, or meticulous enough for her or the internal judge I had adopted. The light, energy, and vibration of my bright
spirit was diverted to the task of pre-empting what I perceived as my
mother's expectations. When I was 21 my mother passed away from
complications due to diabetes, and I, still alive, was wishing she had
taken me with her.

Even before my mother's death, I learned to hide behind my smile,
pretending my heart wasn't broken. The child inside grew with me,
curled up with good books, enjoyed too much good food, and mastered
the art of "staying under the radar." The external adult went on with
life, gathering tools, finishing degrees, getting jobs, marrying my best
friend, and being "successful" in the world. All the while, I put the pur-
poseful dreams of my innate self on-hold, while I focused on surviving.
Depression eroded the life-affirming core inside me, and I believed I
was inherently flawed. It had gotten to the point where I stopped looking people in the eye. I just wanted to hide myself away forever.

During these years, I felt as if I was living inside one of those huge "animal suits" like the ones people wear who work at amusement parks. I was
dressed up like a caricature of myself, a big head on a fake body. I had
disappeared inside of an ill-fitting costume, inside layers of protection,
because I believed the person I had become was inherently unworthy
and unlovable. That animal suit just got thicker and thicker and bigger
and bigger, while somewhere buried within was the real me—that girl
full of light and love, getting smaller and smaller and hiding deeper and
deeper inside.

From about the age of seven, I had in one way or another been a caregiver to my mother through her long struggle with diabetes. In my 20s

and 30s, I became a caregiver to my father during his challenges with diabetes and Parkinson's. From daily errands, doctors' appointments, taking care of the house, being a care advocate, fighting with the health care system, and literally nursing wounds (common to diabetes), I thoroughly learned what it is to give all of oneself for another.

Much like the long, slow decline of my both of my parents, the next two decades saw a gradual collapse of my own health. The less I did to care for myself, the less effective I was at making time to care for myself. I dedicated myself to long hours at work, finishing to-do's, answering emails, getting projects done, and managing teams. My life battery was draining dangerously low as I pushed on for others. At the end of 16-20 hour days at my corporate job, I'd drag myself into my house and crawl up my stairs to fall asleep in my bed, fully clothed. On some occasions I barely made it to the downstairs sofa where I would collapse. My body was overloaded with physical and emotional weight and toxins. My mind was a sieve, unable to remember the smallest detail or the most recent activities, and my spirit was in tatters from succumbing to the belief of "not being enough…"

At the age of 39 I felt 89. I found myself at the end of the long rope I'd let out over decades of being of service to others at the expense of myself. One night, as I lay exhausted on the sofa, staring vacantly into space, I realized I had a choice to sacrifice myself with the noose around my neck, or untie the loop and use the rope to pull myself up over the precipice.

In that realization, it also occurred to me that I had become focused on the short-term goal of making it through the day ahead of me, never considering the long-term goal of surviving at all. Ironically, this was my way of "living in the moment." As a result of my short-sightedness, my spirit was desiccated, detached, and despairing. I felt like I was dying, and for all intents and purposes, I was. Little did I realize that my metaphysical death was immanent, and that death was necessary for me to be re-born.

Around my 40th birthday, a series of revelations brought a gradual dawn upon me: I had fulfilled the arduous contract my soul had made to "be there" for my parents in this life. Now I had an opportunity to show up for myself—and I made that exact choice to consciously commit to supreme self-care. I decided I was going to live my life with renewed purpose and dedication to reviving my energetic life-force. This didn't mean I was never going to be of assistance or service to anybody else, but first and foremost, I needed to care for my Self in the way that only I could.

I made a pact with myself to start aging backwards. I dedicated myself to regaining my youth and with it the freedom to express the unique Light that had naturally shone through me as a child. It was time to take my innate essence off the shelf of my heart, pick her up where I had left her behind, and let her know I would protect her. Now it was safe to be here, and I would do everything I could for her to support her in coming out of the shadows.

I knew that radical and immediate change was necessary—no more excuses, no more distractions, no more justifications. I was literally running out of time. To make matters worse, my doctor informed me that my old analog scale was giving me a ten-pound credit. The day after my doctor's appointment, I purchased a new digital scale, forced my toes onto the cold glass, and held my breath for the numbers to settle, only to find that I was fifteen pounds heavier than my worst day ever! My heart skipped a beat, time slowed down, and I felt like I was falling through the abyss in a dream screaming, "*Nooooooooo*……."

The following week, I resigned from my position at work and took a consulting role that afforded me the time I needed to take care of myself. It was as if a light switch turned on inside of a long tunnel, at the other end was that dear young girl waiting in my heart. Inspired by my leap into the unknown, I decided to take on a personal challenge. I was turning 40, turning over a new leaf, and almost turning over in my grave, so I registered for the Bay to Breakers, an annual 12K race in San Francisco, less than a month away. I had no idea how to prepare for the event, let alone make the huge and lasting changes I needed to make to last the rest of my life. I had no idea a pedicure the next afternoon would change my direction forever.

I walked into a local nail salon for something easy and pampering to literally get me started on the "right foot." As my nails were drying, my conversation with the woman next to me began with the weather and moved synchronistically to self-care, and to both of our experiences with acupuncture. When I told her I wanted to find a new acupuncturist; she highly recommended a local practitioner. The woman and I went our separate ways and I headed home, shaking with the premonition that a life-changing shift was about to happen. A voice inside whispered, *"There's no turning back now."* I recognized this later as the adventurous excitement on which my inner spirit thrives.

Scared of impending judgment and recriminations for having let my health get so bad, I called the acupuncturist's office and scheduled the next available appointment. At our first meeting, I found a kind, wise, compassionate, and hopeful professional. He gifted me a session with the nutritionist on his team and recommended I do a "Spring Cleanse." For 21 days I would eat only natural (unprocessed) foods and take selected organic supplements to clear toxins and inflammation. I returned home with a renewed sense of promise and a new feeling of support that these people could and would help me reunite with my true self. That night, I slept better than I had in months, maybe even years.

Upon meeting the nutritionist, she looked me up and down, and I knew the look of concern on her face was equal to the one of terror on mine. I was afraid I'd fail and end up just like my parents, with slow, long, drawn-out illnesses that drained them of their strength, vitality, and wonder, long before they actually died. The Spring Cleanse was going to be a challenge and an expense I hadn't planned on. At the same time, it was a self-investment opportunity I couldn't turn down. Sobbing, I told my husband what I was considering. Between the tears, he got the gist and said, *"We're in this together. If you want to do the cleanse, I'm doing it with you!"*

The cleanse was a jumpstart, and exactly what I needed to get my body back on track, to clear my mind, and revive my spirit. The physical symptoms of detox were like a freight train, and many a day was spent on that same sofa I had come to appreciate. Emotionally, the cleanse replenished my sense of hope and spurred me to keep progressing forward. My husband and I both released extra physical weight we had been carrying, and with it, long-held emotional heaviness as well.

I had known about the Bay to Breakers since I was a kid and never in a million years thought I could ever be fit enough to do it. As race day approached, I took the saying to heart, *"What doesn't kill you makes you stronger."* Because I wasn't properly conditioned for the task ahead, I started preparing for "damage control." Three days prior to the race I started dosing with ibuprofen to block my pain receptors. I bought a disposable hot pack for my stiff and chronically pained back. I found an old fanny pack to carry water and food because my fluids, nutrients, and energy systems were still out of whack. I also packed extra ibuprofen, anti-histamines, and topical analgesics to ward off the pain I knew was coming.

I barely survived the Bay to Breakers, and I couldn't have done it without the help of two friends who patiently paced me for over three and a half hours, and my determined spirit who walked encouragingly beside me, telling me I could finish and would triumph. After the race, my skin was raw from chaffing and burned from the hot pack on my back. Everything hurt. I couldn't walk the next day, or the day after that, but I managed a stroll on the third day, and little farther each day after. My playful nature had gotten a taste of the physical activity she missed, and in time this taste would become a healthy craving. I've walked/jogged the Bay to Breakers the third Sunday in May, every year since, as an anniversary, a reminder and as an embodied memorial. (God Bless that woman who was me; may she be free of all that pain, fear, and self-loathing forever.)

By the middle of July, my husband wanted to join a gym. I knew I needed to, and…I just wasn't feeling it. But he had done the cleanse with me, so the least I could do was go to the gym with him. By August, I was bored silly with my workouts and looking for more variety. In my youth, I had been a "gym rat," but all the years of body-issues had stripped away the pleasure of movement and the last thing I wanted was for people to be looking at me. As it turned out, nobody looked at me. I, however, found myself watching the other gym-goers, some dedicated to working hard and some more interested in socializing.

In the crowd, one person stood out, a trainer who worked with all kinds of people, not just the ones who looked like they didn't need to be there. He had his clients doing all kinds of different exercises, and it seemed like more fun than a repetitive routine. I mustered up the courage to schedule a training session. He took it easy on me, but I didn't even make it through the first half-hour before I almost passed out. Like an old car engine, even after a good cleansing, I wasn't quite ready to "hit the open road."

That first session told me everything I needed to know: after one session, I felt more like myself than I had in twenty years, and that was precisely what all of me wanted and needed more of. I knew with unwavering certainty that whatever the future held, it was going to have all of me in it, the whole me I always knew was inside, the "me" who was waiting and ready to come out of that old animal suit once and for all! My spirit was ready to take up the energetic space necessary to be myself, without taking up the extra physical space I had previously been hiding behind.

I won't say this transformation was easy. Dying to our old ways never is. I discovered "It takes a village." I progressively created a team and a web of people who supported me in being healthy and fully embodying the many facets of my character. I worked with professionals who could mirror a vibrant life back to me. These people believed that no matter what I looked like, no matter how I showed up, I was showing up the best I could, as much as I could, and they held the vision of what was possible for me when I couldn't hold it for myself.

One of the side effects of this was that I lost 60 pounds. I was relieved to have released the physical weight, but even when the physical weight dissolved, I still thought of myself as "not good enough." It almost didn't matter that my body looked different because I still felt like I had sacrificed both the years of my youth and the energy of my spirit. I believed I wasn't inherently capable of seeing my dreams fully manifest. I still thought that everyone else saw me the way that I used to view myself, and there was still a huge split in my psyche. I had spent so many years ashamed of living in my personal animal suit that I suffered from chronic wounds deep below the skin. It turned out that those wounds have been more of a challenge to overcome than the weight.

It has taken time for me to shift my mindset and my underlying emotions, and ultimately through many cycles of metamorphosis, the very cells of my body. Ultimately, however, this path led me to my personal Renaissance, a re-birth to my Authentic Self, which sends me a message clear and true: *"You are inherently worthy because of the being you are, not because of what you can do for other people."*

In 2009, I made a commitment to myself to heal my body, mind, heart, spirit, and soul. Five years and six Bay to Breakers later, my body is strong. Yes, it's still thicker than I'd like, and… I am the most fit and athletic I've ever been. YET. Every year I have gotten healthier, stronger, more energetic, more vibrant, more joyous, more centered, more aligned, more congruent, more "me," and I intend to be saying that every year onward, from a place in my heart where spirit, body, and mind are integrated and aligned.

Even today, and forward from this time, I know I am a "work-in-progress." I am empowered to be more of my Self, and less of who everyone else expects me to be. I've come a long way, and I'm proud of that! I can now say, *"I love who I am, because I am me."* As an evolution-in-progress, I see more shifts ahead, and however my life unfolds, I say *"yes"* to opportunities to be more fully the person I inherently am, one who manifests the ageless Light of my Spirit and has given new life to the joyful child within. That is why I am Laura Diana Lopez, Renaissance Woman. I have been re-born to my Self, and I believe in that renaissance for you.

———————•◦•———————

Laura Diana Lopez, M.A., is a dynamic and motivated force of nature, who's passionate about living a nourishing life. Her life-long commitment to personal evolution is evidenced by both her extensive education, and her depth and breadth of practice in body-mind-spirit modalities. Certifications in Intuitive Energy Medicine, Conscious Bodywork, Reiki, Yin Yoga and Holistic Health Coaching, combined with her advanced degrees in psychology give her a multi-faceted approach to transformation.

Her twenty-five years of front-line professional experience in corporate cultures bring every-day practicality to making enduring change. Laura stands for raising conscious awareness as a model for moving through life. From this model, she is authoring her book, "The Transformative Practice of Choice." Laura Diana Lopez is a Renaissance Woman, who has firsthand experience of reinventing herself and her life. When Laura isn't writing, speaking or coaching, you'll find her cooking in the kitchen, or on the open road for a photo-shoot, manifesting the essence and art of life! For more information about Laura go to her website www.lauradianalopez.com, and to see her Art of Life™, visit her online photo gallery at www.manifessence.com.

Permission Granted

"The thing that is really hard, and really amazing, is giving up on being perfect and beginning the work of becoming yourself."
Anna Quindlen

Dr. Samantha Madhosingh

The first time I read this quote from Anna Quindlen, it really struck a chord. I had spent so much of my life attempting to be perfect and found myself wondering just what it would be like to live a life without any facades, without any masks, and without pretending. What would it really be like to give myself permission to just be me and not believe I had to be perfect all the time? What would people think of me if they knew the real me? What would they say? Would I be accepted? Did it really matter what other people thought of me? But then, what would I think of myself?

You see, there is a very big difference between accepting yourself as whole, perfect, and complete as the person who you are, and desiring to be perfect, infallible, and free from ever making a mistake. The former is empowering, energizing, and fulfilling, and the latter can be the source of much distress and a life filled with fear.

The fascinating thing about being a perfectionist is that there is an entrenched belief that being perfect, not making mistakes and being flawless, is actually possible. Perfectionists believe that success can happen without failure, without missteps, without disappointment. They believe that perfection is the only way to deserve love and acceptance. In other words, if people were to see your flaws, they would see that you were not good enough to be loved and accepted.

You see, at its root, striving for perfection and wanting to be perfect is ingrained in the desire to believe we are worthy of love and the wish to feel like we belong. A sense of belonging fuels our basic need to know that we are a part of something much larger than ourselves. We believe we belong when we allow ourselves to be vulnerable, without masks, showing whom we truly are, and we are embraced and accepted completely.

Belonging is fundamental to our sense of happiness and wellbeing, and without it intense feelings of loneliness and distress can result. Because our human need for love, connection, and belonging is so critical to our happiness, it often gets tied to meeting the approval of others. In many instances, people grow up to be approval-seeking perfectionists because they believe that the only way to receive acceptance, love, and belonging is to live a perfect life and with so-called perfect behavior.

Unfortunately, striving for a life without mistakes is folly because it is impossible to be perfect and right all the time. What I have also realized is that insisting on perfection is crippling and can affect your career as well as your relationships. In your career, it can start with the premise of *"If I can't do it perfectly, then I won't do it at all,"* leading to a life of procrastination and stress from missed deadlines. And, I can assure you that if you are an entrepreneur and running your own business, there are so many unknowns and a lot of mistakes will be made along the way. So if you are afraid of being wrong and believe you can't make mistakes, you will never allow yourself to be open to trying new things.

Being afraid to fail will stop you in your tracks and neither you nor your business will grow. And, most of all, being a perfectionist is stressful and exhausting. It leaves you with little energy to truly live the life you want.

In relationships, perfectionists expect everyone else around them to be perfect too. It is hidden behind the concept of having "high standards." But that's really code for perfection. And, the problem is these "standards" are impossible to attain or maintain, so they are frequently disappointed. Perfectionists have a strong tendency to focus on the negative so they find it easier to point out the mistakes and errors made rather than strengths. They also struggle with accepting responsibility for their own actions because acknowledging they have done something wrong or made a mistake is unbearable.

As a perfectionist, judgment, criticism, and being in control underscore relationships with others. This means that being in any kind of relationship with someone who is a perfectionist ends up meaning that you too will never feel good enough. So, if you are the husband, wife, partner, son, daughter, brother, sister, friend, employee, or have some other connection to someone who is a perfectionist, you may feel that it is impossible to come anywhere close to meeting their expectations of you, and they have the belief that you are just not good enough. And, if you are a parent, as I am, just imagine what it might be like to be the child of someone who is a perfectionist. Is it okay to make mistakes? Does your child know that they are whole, perfect, and complete just the way they are?

Living life in search of perfection sounds untenable, doesn't it? Yet so many people (myself included for a long time) live under the pretense that they can create a perfect life with the perfect job, the perfect relationship, the perfect house filled with perfect children, and a nice perfect car sitting in the driveway. They believe that once they have all of this, they will be happy. But life is messy and challenging; disappointments, failures and mistakes can litter it. It is through all of these lessons that we grow and ultimately succeed in living a full life.

What I have also observed from the many people I work with is that having the seemingly perfect job or career, the seemingly perfect relationship, with the seemingly perfect kids, and the seemingly perfect stuff is not a particularly reliable measure for happiness. There are so many people with a life that looks good on paper and yet they are miserable. Happiness, then, does not result from being perfect.

Let me tell you a story.

As a girl I learned that I had arrived into this world purely by accident. I was the result of two teenagers with raging hormones. I was not the child my parents had longingly dreamed of and purposely created. Once I learned this truth when I was 12 years old, my mind began to tell me that I was a mistake. I didn't belong. I wasn't really wanted or deeply loved. I didn't deserve to be here. I believed I needed to be perfect to earn my place in the world and to earn the love and respect of the people I loved. It felt overwhelming and impossible. I spent years fueling myself with this lie, and it was devastating. I was depressed for most of my adolescence and found little enjoyment in the world around me. Who could ever love me if I was mistakenly here? Could I ever be perfect enough to be loved? I wanted to run far, far, away. But what I realized later was that no matter how far I ran I would always catch up with myself. I would never be able to outrun me.

In college and as an adult, I realized that I knew how to "act perfect" to give the impression that all was well with me, and I had it all together. This led to relationships with men who had that expectation of me. They put me on a pedestal and had the expectation of me being "perfect" all the time. I found myself constantly afraid of making a mistake or of us having a disagreement because whenever I veered from the path they expected of me, I was treated as though I was unlovable and unacceptable.

This validated for me that I had to be perfect to be loved, and I could never be accepted just for being myself. I continued to berate myself whenever I deemed my actions to be imperfect (which was often). Every mistake I made, every misstep and failure, would send my conscience into overdrive focusing on all that was wrong with me, which meant I shouldn't be here. Inside my head was this maddening conflict. I knew how to "act perfect" but I also knew that I wasn't really perfect, and this was intolerable.

Early on in graduate school, a relationship that I was deeply emotionally invested in with someone who wanted and expected me to be perfect began to come to an end, and I began to fall apart. Because I was studying psychology, I recognized the signs that I was sliding very quickly in a very deep depression. My pretense of being the perfect student unraveled as I couldn't keep up with my work, and I began to withdraw into my own little world. For months and months I tormented myself and could not get back on my feet. I barely did what I needed to do to get by, but I couldn't concentrate or focus on my schoolwork. Eventually, they attempted to terminate me from the program. And, while their actions felt like an incredible betrayal for a number of reasons, I have since come to realize they actually did me a huge favor. Their actions forced me to fight for myself and complete the program. But it also left a deep and lasting fear of failure.

Every step of the way in my career as a psychologist, I felt I had something to prove. I had to prove I was worthy of the degree that had my name on it. I had to prove that no one had done me any favors. I had to prove they were wrong about me. I had to prove I wasn't a fraud. And, I wanted to prove that I would not just be a good psychologist, but I would be a great psychologist. I remember studying for the psychologist licensing exam for months and believing that if I did not pass the first time that this would confirm that I was not good enough to be a psychologist. When I think about it now, it sounds pretty ridiculous the amount of pressure I put on myself. But, I still remember coming out of that exam and calling my mother practically in tears, convinced I had failed. For weeks I was miserable, thinking I was a failure and didn't deserve to be helping people. Receiving that license in the mail was so incredible. I saw it as validation that I was on the right path and was "good enough" to be a psychologist. And, although I did pass the licensing exam the first time, it would take many more years for me to fully move beyond the feeling that I was a big fraud.

Earlier, I described that being a perfectionist means being able to "act perfect" and believing that there is such a thing as living a mistake-free life. And, while I was really the poster child for a messy and imperfect life, as most of us really are, I continued to allow the impression to build that I was perfect. It concerned me because it felt disingenuous and inauthentic.

My clients frequently told me they experienced me as "being perfect" or that I must have had an easy life or a "perfect" life, as they put it, or that I appeared to be a "perfect parent". And, while I always told them that I wasn't perfect by a long shot, I never explained that I had been on my own very long journey to where I was emotionally, what I had been through to get there, or that I continue to work on myself each and every day. What I also didn't tell them is that I really knew what they were going through. I knew what depression was like. I knew what it felt like to be suicidal, to feel hopeless and helpless, and I also knew what it was like to take medication. As a psychologist, we were not supposed to ever talk about our personal lives or past, but it troubled me that I was holding onto this secret.

After spending some time being still and in prayer, it came to me that I needed to tell my story. I needed to come clean about my life experiences with depression, and the impact it had on my life. I needed to be empowered by my journey of overcoming, not feel ashamed by it. I wanted to embrace the whole person who I am and not have to hide pieces of myself. And so I gave myself permission to present my imperfections to the world by writing my eBook, "Magnify Your Brilliance: 5 Keys to a Powerful Life." It was nerve wracking. I was terrified that presenting my imperfect self for all to see would render me unacceptable. As afraid as I was, I knew I had to do it so that I could overcome the paralyzing fear of failure as well as the nagging feeling that I was a fraud.

Writing my story was such a blessing. I no longer feel like a fraud, living with the fear that somehow, someway, someday, someone would find out my secret. I "outed" myself by telling the world I had suffered from depression. It was incredibly freeing as I was no longer at the mercy of my fears. What I also realized is that it has made me much more relatable to the people I work with and even to those who have only read my book. For me, writing that book was when I finally granted myself the permission I needed to live my life fully and pursue progress along my life journey and not perfection. I have realized that making a mistake is not fatal and each lesson helps me grow.

Here are some of the things I have discovered that assist in the journey of recovering from perfectionism:

1. **Nurture Self-Love:** According to Brene' Brown in her book, "The Gifts of Imperfection," *"Love is not something we give or get; it is something that we nurture and grow, a connection that can only be cultivated between two people when it exists within each one of them—we can only love others as much as we love ourselves."* I would also add that we show other people how to love us by the way we treat ourselves. So when we practice self-love and treat ourselves lovingly, we invite them to do the same. It is therefore vital that we discover how to love ourselves completely and unconditionally.

   Practice embracing who you are, realizing that in order to be worthy of love all you have to do is be you. You are deserving and good enough simply because you are. Nurture the fledgling love you have inside for yourself. As we raise children, we teach them the importance of loving everyone other than themselves. It's no wonder we grow up without a clue about how to do this.

Spend some quiet time thinking about your strengths, all the qualities you love about yourself. If this is difficult for you, sit with a friend or loved one and ask them to describe for you all the things they love about you. Your job is to simply sit and listen and allow yourself to absorb the things they are telling you without interrupting or contradicting what they are saying. When they are finished, write down what you remember them saying. Alternatively, you may consider recording the session and then listening to it afterwards and taking notes.

2. **Develop Positive Self-Talk**: People often tell me they are trying to be more positive in the way they live their lives, but as soon as they start talking about themselves they begin using all these negative words. Our words are so very powerful and have a meaningful impact in the way we live our lives.

What you tell yourself all day long is what you become. In many instances, if we spoke to our friends in the manner in which we speak constantly to ourselves, no one would speak to us ever again. When we use negatively charged words, we don't always realize the power those words have on our energy, our outlook, how we feel about ourselves, and how we treat others. Practice using positively focused words to describe yourself and your life.

Seeing my life as a miracle, rather than a mistake, was much more energizing and empowering and meant that I could be loveable and perfect just the way I am. Positive self-talk is an important tool in retraining your brain to be more positively focused, thus creating new neuro-pathways. You are the master of your mind. You have the power to change the way you think and on what you choose to focus your attention.

3. **Live a Life of Gratitude**: It is so much easier to be grateful when things are going well, and you feel you are happy. But living a life of gratitude means appreciating each and every day and circumstance that occurs no matter what. Begin and end each day with moments of gratitude. Create a gratitude list to help you focus on all the things that you do have in your life rather than on what's lacking, missing, or perceived to not be right. Be grateful that you are alive and have the ability to create a second chance for yourself.

4. **Learn to Forgive**: Holding on to anger, grudges, and blaming others creates a build-up of toxic emotions that doesn't serve you. One of the most important things you will ever do in life is learn how to forgive. Forgiveness is critical to healing, but one of the most difficult things to do. Many people find they have trouble with forgiving because they equate forgiveness with absolving the other person or persons of responsibility for their actions. Forgiving someone for their actions isn't really about them. It's all about you. It means removing the power that the situation or circumstances has over you so you can be free to experience life fully in the present moment and enjoy forming healthy new connections with people and situations that are uplifting and supportive.

5. **Engage in Fun, Play, & Laughter:** Celebrate yourself and your life. Of all the people in our lives, it is children who seem to be the happiest. Have you ever wondered why that might be? Most children just simply love to engage in playtime activities that are fun, and they know how to laugh. As we grow older, we have a tendency to give up on the idea of having fun and replace it with being responsible. A 40-something-year-old woman recently mentioned to me that she had an A-HA moment and realized that she had given up on the one thing she really enjoyed doing...dancing. I asked her why she had

stopped. She said she didn't know exactly why but knew that she needed to get back to it. Often as we get older, we think we should no longer do those fun things we used to enjoy in our youth. Why not? Life is for living and enjoying. Let your creative side shine and flow, and have some fun.

I have discovered that no matter how you were conceived, your very presence on this earth is, in fact, a miracle. When you think about the randomness of biology, you realize that the fact that any of us are created and have survived the entire process from conception, pregnancy, childbirth, and through childhood is incredible. Our presence, no matter how we got here, is divinely inspired and beautiful. We all have purpose to our lives and we are here for good reason. And we may spend a lifetime trying to figure out that reason, but there are no mistakes in the creation of life. Tomorrow isn't promised, so spend today filling your life with love.

In reality, you don't have to be "perfect" (meaning without error or mistake) to be worthy of love. You don't have to be perfect to be good enough to receive love. And the real truth is that in our imperfections, we simply are perfect. Give yourself permission to simply be you, whoever that is. Love yourself with wild abandon. Open your heart to new possibilities and realize that the truest legacy of your life will be the connections you have with the people around you. Live the life you want by creating a life you simply love with no facades, no masks, and no pretending.

Our life journeys are all different and yet we all essentially want the same thing. We want to know that we matter, that we belong, that we are loved. I want you to realize, right in this moment, that this is true for you. You matter, you belong, and you are loved. Think about what you wish for your life and all that you are blessed with. As you awaken to who you are truly meant to be and embrace the full essence of you, you will intuitively know that you are whole, perfect, and complete.

———————•◆•———————

Dr. Samantha Madhosingh, known as America's "Holistic Success Doctor®" shows you how to find deep fulfillment and happiness in every single area of your life. Teaching people how to *Strike it Happy™*, she believes that happiness has nothing to do with luck and everything to do with how you view the world, plus your desire and willingness to boldly live out loud. Having spent over 15 years studying the connections between mind, body, and spirit, Dr. Samantha uses practical techniques for change, including advanced cognitive therapy and positive psychology approaches, which will help you change your thinking (and life) forever.

Dr. Samantha received her PsyD. in psychology from The George Washington University and is a clinical psychologist, speaker and sought after expert in emotional wellness, happiness, fulfillment, love, relationships and holistic success.

A frequent media contributor and sought-after expert for both local and national media, she has appeared on FOX, NBC, CBS, Emotional MoJo, Daytime and Heart & Soul. She is the author of *Magnify Your Brilliance: 5 Keys To A Powerful Life* and her latest book *Strike It Happy: 101 Reflections to Revolutionize Your Life* will be published Fall, 2014.

Making herself accessible to the public through her newly launched online show "Ask Dr. Samantha," she answers tough questions on love, happiness, fulfillment, self-sabotage, breakthroughs, motivation, living fearlessly, finding your inner power and rekindling the spark in all of your relationships.

Dr. Samantha is a successful businesswoman and devoted mother. She loves exploring the world with her daughter and engaging in the wonderful journey of motherhood. To find about more about her go to www.AskDrSamantha.com

Who Me, Shine?

Rebecca Hall Gruyter

Have you ever felt that pull, that excitement, that pressure as if the spotlights are focused on you and you're being called to step forward and stand out—to say *"yes?"* To share more of whom you are and in fact SHINE! And if you're anything like me, my first gut response was *"Who—me? Are you sure you have the right person?"* I looked around to see if perhaps they meant the person behind me, only to realize, yes, they actually meant me. Then my response was fear.

Who Me?

I've felt it many times in my life—this pull, this call to step forward in some way. Sometimes feeling a pull to serve, or to lead, or to help, or to support—which I could do. The leading was a bit scary, but when I was called to step forward and shine—to share more fully who I was and not hide behind information or a role—saying *"yes"* was one of the most terrifying, life-altering, and powerful decisions I have ever made. I was asked to say *"yes"* to sharing my story wherever and whenever I was called to do so—without rules, without holding back, without hiding—regardless of the platforms, mediums, and/or stages I was called to share my story. It was also one of the most wonderful and freeing decisions I have ever made. I find it interesting how freedom, purpose, and fulfillment are frequently just on the other side of fear.

Going back to fear and decisions, in the past when I was asked to step forward in a bigger way than I had before—to share more of me in a more vulnerable way, or to lead in a new way, or just plain stand out in any way—I would shrink back. I would ask, *"Who—me? Who am I to help with this?"* I could quickly list all of the ways I was not qualified and who was much better qualified—even when, sometimes if I really listened closely, there was a small hopeful part of me that longed to say *"yes"*—I just felt so unworthy and unqualified as I could so quickly and powerfully see where I lacked. Until I learned a powerful truth: that we are perfect in our imperfections.

Perfect in Our Imperfections

We can serve and make a difference by just being willing, saying *"yes."* When the pull and call comes, I've learned to trust that if I'm called, I'm exactly what's needed for such a time as this—imperfections and all. I can trust God to fill in the gaps…if my heart is willing. He won't let me fall, but will serve through me—especially when I know I'm imperfect and can lean on Him to enable me to shine, lead, and serve. I have a choice to say *"yes"* or *"no"*—that I could choose to live a life on purpose and with a purpose, honoring and celebrating the unique way I am gifted and made.

Can I share with you some of my story? The parts of my journey that have been laid on my heart and I believe I've been asked to share with you because I believe it's not an accident you were drawn to this book and have elected to read my chapter. I believe that there is something in these words and from my heart for you to serve and support you on your journey. So, please open your heart and listen to the message or messages that are just for you.

Open Your Heart and Listen

My story doesn't start with someone many view as fearless and a dynamic international Radio Talk Show Host, listened to on the Empowerment Channel of VoiceAmerica, or a Best Selling Author, Motivational Speaker, Empowerment Leader, someone who will stand, share, and shine to serve her people, a Business Coach, or an Award Winning Financial Professional, or the Creator of Your Success Formula™ or even the Creator of the Speaker Talent Search. It starts much more humbly with a little girl just 6 years old who learns her parents are getting a divorce.

She didn't quite know what that meant except that Daddy wouldn't be coming home anymore. This was crushing to the little girl, as Daddy was her hero.

For the next six years, this little girl was thrust into an environment of abuse that no one saw or believed. She experienced abuse, pain, neglect, mental and physical and sexual abuse, hurt and intense fear—never feeling safe, heard, protected, or believed. Experiencing things a little girl should never experience, feel, or see. Those that she should have been able to trust to save and protect her instead harmed, betrayed, and harmed her. So from this she learned the following lessons: *"It's my fault. Something is wrong with me; I'm not okay. I'm not valuable or lovable. It's not safe. I can't trust. I don't matter."* And ultimately, *"It's not safe to be seen or heard."*

You see, I know the painful walk of this young girl because, you see, I was this young girl—formed, built, and molded in this difficult environment during my formative years.

I was eventually rescued from this environment and moved in with my Birth Father (my Daddy) and my Stepmother, who became the "mother of my heart." As I began my healing journey, I learned some new deeper truths that helped me discover my original beliefs were actually horrible lies. I then got to choose to believe truth over lies, but the choice was mine. The truths I learned were that I was actually lovable, had great value, that I was (and actually all of us are) and am beautifully and wonderfully made, on purpose and with a purpose, and ultimately that it was safe to be seen and heard. That being seen and sharing my voice no longer put me in serious danger. But I/we have a choice to live in fear of the past or move forward on purpose and with purpose.

Choose to Believe Truth over Lies

A choice lies within us—a choice with each breath to believe in the truth and to live life on purpose, or to choose to believe the lies and even repeat them. We frequently can't choose the circumstances or events that happen to us. However, we can choose our response and how we elect to be. I could have stayed a hurt little girl, a victim, and repeat the cycle, but instead I chose to believe the truth and live my life on purpose and with purpose being and becoming how I ultimately am and want to be.

On my journey, I learned a lot about fear and stepping through it. Just because I could start to see the truth and believe it over the lies doesn't mean it wasn't scary and difficult to step forward and build a life based on this new belief system. Each step in the journey stretched me. Each time I stretched into a new area or shared more of me, I faced fear. In high school and college, it was a courageous act for me to stand up in front of two or more people and say my name, much less answer a question. You see, my body would remember what went on before and would try to protect me and shut me down—losing my words, shaking, and losing my voice as my throat would close down to prevent a voice or words from coming out—as if I was still in danger if I was seen or heard. Every time I was called on in class or at work to lead teams or step forward in some additional way, it was a courageous act and took facing and stepping into and through fear when I was called to share the truth and confront the abusers with it. Courage, I think, is not an absence of fear, but still doing what you're called to do even when afraid. This is a courageous act.

Courageous Acts

Growing up in a very difficult, abusive environment where it was literally not safe and then being removed from that, where I moved into a new environment that allowed me to heal and bloom and grow. I discovered that it *could be safe,* and it was important for me to bloom and grow, that I *did* matter and could make a difference just by being me. But I will tell you it was terrifying every time I stood up because my body on a cellular level still remembered what went on before. So I would experience fear at levels where most people I talked to would not experience fear on the level that I did. Just to stand up and say my name in class or to connect with somebody on a real level was a really, really difficult, fearful, terrifying thing for me to face repeatedly

I felt a similar fear every time I stood up in class and shared, or led a team, or gave a presentation, or stood in front of an audience or in front of a camera or a recording device. Yet, I also discovered that I survived every time and got a little less afraid and a little more confident. I learned I wasn't in mortal danger, that I could trust myself and God. I started to become less afraid of fear and started to learn fear is just a warning system that I'm treading somewhere I haven't been before, that's all—that this is new territory and we don't know if we can survive because we haven't done it before. Typically, we feel fear when it's not a life threatening situation, but we feel the emotion as if we were in mortal danger. The trick I've learned is to lean into the feeling, not away from it:

1. Check to see if you are in true danger; if so, remove yourself from the situation.
2. If you're not in true danger, then lean in and realize you're stretching and growing—all good things.

As I learned to do this, I came to understand that frequently the fear I was feeling was an indication of growth. In this way, fear became my friend.

I've learned that if I'm continuing to grow and stretch, then I will feel this emotion of fear frequently. Now, I know if I'm feeling fear and am afraid, then it's an indicator that I'm stretching and growing. It's okay to be afraid, just don't let it stop you. It's a sign you're growing. What's your courageous act? A way you can step out and through your fear?

Let Fear Become Your Friend

It was a courageous act for me to seek help when I needed it. To be vulnerable, authentic, and willing to let others hear and see me. It was a courageous and terrifying *"yes"* when I elected to say *"yes"* and share my story for the first time—and many times after. To say *"yes"* to lead my community, to being interviewed on radio shows, television shows, write books, and speak. However, it has also become a joyful act even when I'm being stretched and get to face fear and growth along the way.

I do a lot of live events and retreats, seminars and classes, and one of the common things I'm asked about is fear because so many people view me as someone who is fearless. Or how do I just keep going when things get hard? And it's so interesting to me that many perceive me as fearless and unstoppable. One friend describes me as "a force to be reckoned with." I think this is because I'm all in, a *"yes"* to stepping forward and sharing and giving as I'm called to give, regardless of fear. What they may not understand is I'm frequently dancing with fear, but I don't let it stop me. So, it's not that I'm fearless, but that I'm committed to facing fear, to leaning in and stepping through to the other side. I think the unstoppable part comes from a willingness to get up again when I fall and skin my knee. I'm here to serve and shine fully in all that I'm called to do—just as I believe you are, too.

I've shared with you how I've gotten intimately acquainted with fear and one of the things I learned about it is that frequently we are experiencing and feeling fear, and we're actually not in mortal danger, even though our mind and body are sometimes sending the signal that we are. I know what it's like to truly be afraid and in true danger and what it's like to feel that way even if it's not reality at times, but can feel like it. That's where leaning in and really stopping and asking the two questions I gave you earlier can be so powerful in helping you move through fear. Many times, as I was starting my speaking career, I would eye the exit because it really helped me to know the escape strategy if I needed it, that I could walk off at any time and that empowered me. I have not elected to walk off stage, but it has been helpful to remember I could and was choosing to stay on stage. Every time I lived through the fear and I stretched a little bit, I became less fearful.

You Get to Choose

I shared with you that fear is really just an emotion, just an experience. It would come up not because I was in mortal danger, but it was because I was stretching into a territory that was new—that my mind and body actually didn't know that I could survive because I hadn't lived through it yet. Once I discovered that secret, I could recognize that the fear was simply trying to protect me, and the more I could see it and have a dialogue almost with it, *"I promise—we know the escape route if we need it. I'm not in mortal danger. I'm here to serve my people, or I'm here to give in this way, or I'm here to share and expand in this way."*

Fear would calm me down a little bit, not shutting it down, not mocking myself because I was afraid, but accepting the fear while assuring myself that I was not in mortal danger. This has given me so much freedom in life that I don't shut down like that anymore. And every new thing that I may have that twinge of fear, I know there are amazing things on the other side, that I'm not in mortal danger, that I'm stretching my wings, that I'm growing. Actually it has translated to an excitement and an anticipation that if I'm **not** feeling that discomfort once in a while or that stretching, then I'm probably not playing big enough.

I have learned the secret dealing with fear and discomfort is actually to lean into it. To honor the fear, but reminding yourself that you're not in mortal danger; that you're stretching and growing. Lean into the discomfort and honor the feeling and then lean through that just on the other side of fear and discomfort is growth, courage, confidence, and empowerment.

Lean Into the Discomfort

The other key thing I've learned is that we have to separate the *"yes"* from the *"how."* So frequently when we feel a call on our heart, a call on our life, our mind starts trying to figure out **how** and then we try to decide if it's a *"yes"* or *"no"* once we figure out 17 plans and ways to get there. I find if we can just get still and pause, then really listen to our body, if it is a *"yes"*—and frequently you'll lean forward, kind of be excited—or if it is a *"no"*—and a lot of times if it is a *"no"*—you're going to push back and feel a weight with a *"no."* What I have found is every time I have honored the *"yes"* fear or *"no"* fear, the *"how"* always falls into place.

I want to invite you to lean in, that you matter, that nobody else can share your story, can lead in the way that you are called to lead. You, fully being you, matters. It makes a huge difference, and I want to invite you to not hide parts of yourself, whatever it may be. I'm inviting you to be willing to bring *all* of you forward into your life and share fully all that you are. *You* are a gift! Share yourself and all of whom you are with those around you.

You Are the Gift

Regarding fear, it is your choice to let fear stop you or to lean in and step through the fear to the other side. Many people wait hoping they will feel more "comfortable" later or less fearful or more prepared. Yet while they're waiting, everyone around them misses out! And they find when they *do* finally decide to take that step forward, that they are still afraid and uncomfortable. So the waiting didn't lessen the fear; it just delayed it—they still had to face it.

Every time I have been willing to face my fear, people have been impacted just by how I showed up. Please understand, I have been privileged to impact and inspire others simply because I was willing, not because I have some special unattainable qualifications. It's because I'm willing to share fully, perfect in my imperfections (a work-in-progress) and letting go and letting God fill in the rest and serve through me. I believe He calls the imperfect vessels to serve, that He is able to perfectly serve through a work-in-progress like me and like you. But, it takes a willing heart, willing to be vulnerable and imperfect.

Think about those people who have impacted you, made you smile, lifted your spirit just by how they walk their walk. Just by the way they shared themselves and their life with you. It can be as simple as a smile or a hug. Or them witnessing you taking a stand that is really important to both of you. Having a willingness to serve, make mistakes, and get up and share fully and shine again is a gift and a choice. Once more I say, we all have this opportunity to fully share, serve and shine. We all have this opportunity.

Today–Not Tomorrow, Not Someday–but TODAY

I want you to be a leader in your own life—be in the center stage, not just a supporting character or a role. And I want you to start doing that, or if you are doing it, do it in a bigger, brighter, bolder way TODAY. Not tomorrow. Not someday. But to really take that pause, take that breath. *"How can I bring more of me forward? Am I called to be a leader?"* Capturing your life now —what you are thinking, what you are feeling, how you are living your life—is valuable, and then being willing to share that with others is an amazing gift.

Part of letting yourself impact others is the willingness to say *"yes"* and share more of you. Sometimes this *"I want to make a positive difference in the world; I want to impact people in a positive way, those that are passing through my life versus a negative way."*

"I want to make a difference" can be as simple as extending your hand to somebody. It can be as simple as leaning in and giving a hug. It can be seeing a need and assisting. It can be smiling at somebody. Sharing that which makes you smile, connecting with people. These daily things that we do in our life make a huge difference.

So I ask you, are you willing? Are you willing to share more of you? Are you willing to lean in? Are you willing to fully embrace your *"yes"* and step into it? Are you willing to capture some of your story? The choice is yours. Nobody else can make it for you, nor would you want them to. You are empowered in that very way in how you want to live, how you want to walk, and how you choose to respond and take that next step in your journey.

Here is how I invite you to respond when you're called to step forward in a new way and show up in a bigger more powerful way to shine. I would like you to change the response from *"Who—me, shine?"* To: *"Who am I not to shine? Who am I to not answer this call and pull at my heart?"* I invite you to lean into the fact that if you're being pulled/called to step forward—perfect in your imperfections—then someone right now is waiting for you—to have the gift of you in their life in a bigger and brighter way, perhaps sharing more of you with them. Who are you to say *"no?"*

Remember, there isn't another one of you in reserve to take your place if you don't show up big and shiny enough to be seen and to touch others. You are the gift! So, who are you to ignore the call and pass by the opportunity to share the amazing gift of you with all of us? I want you to share you more fully, brightly, and purposefully in all that you do.

It is not an accident that you were drawn to this book and chapter. It is not an accident that you have read to the end of the chapter. So these questions are for you. Lean in and purposefully decide, *"This is where you want to go. This is who you are going to be in this moment. This is how you are going to shine more brightly and share more of yourself."* Are you a *"YES!?"*

Be a *"YES!"*

I started the chapter with the question: *"Who - me, shine?"* I'm here to share that I learned to say *"yes"* to the call to lean in through the fear and really discover who I am and what I'm called to do. I was willing to be seen, to share, to grow, to fall and get back up again—to be perfect in my imperfections—and when I am called to stretch and shine, I already know my answer now is *"YES!"* Who am I to not share who I am and what I've been given to share? I will give, share, and serve. I hope you also choose to answer the call—that you decide *"yes"* to share the amazing gift of you with all of us. I invite you to lean in and discover all of who you are—to fully share and, yes, shine.

And here is a way to say *"yes"* and to impact others right now as you finish this chapter. Think of a story, think of part of your journey today. Perhaps something came to mind when you were reading this chapter. Next, call a friend, call a family member. Send them an email. Reach out and share your story. Reach out and share part of you. Declare that *"I am taking this step forward."* Let people weave their lives and stories together with yours because connection matters. We make a difference when we let people into the richness of who we are.

No one else can take your place or make the decision for you. The choice is yours. What do you choose to do? In this moment with your next breath, how do you choose to respond and answer the call? Are you willing to share you, perfect in your imperfections? A beautiful work-in-progress (it's okay to not be finished yet—we are all in-progress). I hope and pray you say *"yes"*...because your people are waiting for you!

May you say *"yes"* and always, always bloom where you are planted...and shine! Yes, YOU!

SHINE!

Rebecca Hall Gruyter, founder/Owner of Your Purpose Driven Practice, a Character Code Coach®, Master Trainer, Creator or the

Women's Empowerment Series, a Best Selling Author, Creator of Your Success Formula™, and Owner of a successful private practice. She has grown multiple six figure businesses and practices and has a track record of growing, leading executive teams through complex information to streamline results. She is committed to helping you line up your business with you, your core values, and your passions so that you can impact the world in the unique and wonderful way in which you are gifted.

Rebecca has been featured on many Success Panels, Blog Talk Radio, Entrepreneur Initiative, and is a Radio Talk Show Host on the Empowerment Channel of Voice America. She has over 15 years experience speaking, leading, and empowering others, and has received numerous awards for her empowerment work and sales expertise.

Mrs. Hall Gruyter is also the creator of the powerful Speaker Talent Search where she helps connect powerful and dynamic speakers with Community Leaders looking for speakers for radio, live stages, tele-summits, video and television.

Rebecca recently received the award of Client Coach of the Year for her transformational work. Rebecca wants to help you be seen, heard, and shine! To learn more about Rebecca please visit:

www.YourPurposeDrivenPractice.com or schedule a time to talk with her directly at www.MeetWithRebecca.com

Discovering My Path To Wellness...

And My Work in the World

Cassandra Herbert

What is the inspiration for a life's work? For many people, personal mission arose directly from the struggles they, themselves, faced and overcame. Out of the struggle arose a passion to help others overcome the same challenges.

It was certainly that way for me. My companies, Zest and Harmony Counseling and Just Bee Wellness, arose from the lessons I learned in overcoming health challenges that affected my mood, my physical abilities and stamina, my work performance, and most of all my relationships.

To overcome these challenges I needed to re-examine every aspect of my life—physical, emotional, mental, and spiritual—and make changes that nurtured me and supported my health and growth. I discovered, admitted, and overcame food addictions I'd never dreamed were possible...addictions that are not only common, but the norm in our society.

Most important, with my training as a psychiatric nurse, dealing with both the mind and the body, I realized that I could help others to achieve the same wellness I had discovered.

Here's how it all happened...

For over 10 years I had yeast infections off-and-on, and the older I got the more havoc they had on my system. I was very emotional, irritable, and reactive, especially in my romantic relationships, with bouts of brain-fog complicating matters.

I experienced Seasonal Affective Disorders most winters (of course, living in Rochester in snowy Upstate New York probably contributed to this). In the summer I was optimistic, productive, and more vibrant. In the winter I grew pessimistic, tired, less motivated, and craved sugar and carbs more than in the summer.

Of course, like any addiction, my sugar cravings grew more intense over time. I remember when I first became a nurse I would eat a 4-pack of Reese's peanut butter cups and wash it down with a Mountain Dew or Doctor Pepper. I loved sodas when I was growing up but it wasn't until I was a nurse that I began to drink caffeinated soft drinks. I didn't like the colas, but I needed the caffeine to overcome my increasing bouts of fatigue.

Between this pattern of irritability, fatigue, and short-lived sugar highs, my life started to spiral downward. The man I'd dated since college suddenly ended our 6-year relationship and to cover up my sadness, I went into a spiral of anger. Trying to manage my feelings, I turned even more to comfort foods—sugary treats and carbs—along with a very toxic rebound relationship.

Oh, I was angry. Angry at men, God, religion. I wasn't sleeping, so as a remedy I started working nights at the hospital, keeping busy to avoid my feelings.

As you can see, I was doing nothing to nourish my wellness…

Finally, as they say in the Recovery Movement, I hit bottom—I realized that I just couldn't stand the fatigue anymore. I love my energy and the fatigue was impacting my ability to do all the things I wanted to do. I started asking for suggestions, and a friend recommended an Integrative Medical Doctor to me.

Imagine that! Working in the heart of the mainstream medical world, I had never heard of Integrative Medicine. So I set up an appointment, and it was the best experience ever. She actually spent over an hour talking with me, approaching me as a partner in the collaborative project of rebuilding my health.

Prior to my visit with her I'd started reading "The Yeast Connection" by William Crook and was shocked to see it describing many of the symptoms I was having:

- Recurrent vaginal yeast infections
- PMS
- Sugar craving
- Fatigue
- Feeling "spaced out"
- Constipation
- Dry skin
- Irritability

Point for point, they matched my experience. I knew this must be what I had!

I spoke with the doctor about these symptoms and asked her if I might be having an overgrowth of yeast. She said it could be this, or possibly a thyroid problem. So she ordered a food allergy and sensitivity test and ran some thyroid tests on me, as well as a thyroid scan.

Well, guess what showed up on the food allergy and sensitivity test? Yeast! Yes, that's right—yeast. But, what feeds yeast? Sugar. What had I been eating in large amounts since I was about five years old? Sugar!

As I thought about the test results, I realized they made perfect sense. My love affair with sugar had already caused problems in my life. I remember in college I'd been diagnosed with hypoglycemia. If I didn't eat I would become very irritable and shaky and needed to get food right away. I couldn't focus on anything else, but getting food.

After a lifetime of bombarding my system with sugar, my pancreas was not functioning the way it should. And as a result of my body's inability to manage blood glucose, I had developed an overgrowth of yeast, and it was impacting every aspect of my life.

The doctor told me that the cure was an elimination diet: To starve the yeast, I needed to stop eating concentrated sugar, particularly processed foods that contained sugar, sucrose, fructose, and of course high-fructose corn syrup. Many times a total no-sugar diet, which would be to eliminate fruit, is recommended for the overgrowth of yeast. I did not eliminate fruit.

Of course, I also needed to stop eating all products that contained yeast. As she listed all of the foods that contain yeast, I was stunned at the range of sources—from bread (obvious) to seasonings (who'd have guessed?).

It was a struggle! Because sugar is present in almost every food and in extreme amounts in processed foods, most Americans are addicted to it in some form and some more than others. Withdrawal symptoms can range from strong cravings all the way to headaches, flu-like symptoms, and depression...but that is another chapter in another book.

With my doctor's support, I am happy to say that I eliminated sugar from my diet for about six months and eliminated yeast for about a year. And as I write this chapter today, I haven't had a yeast infection for over 10 years!

Overcoming my own addiction to sugar and overgrowth of yeast taught me the power of foods, and my journey to wellness through nutrition inspired me to assist others in healing. After my work with the Integrative physician, I knew that I wanted to practice as a holistic wellness practitioner, treating clients through assessing what they were eating, how they were sleeping, their stress level, support systems, their relationships, etc., and helping them make healthy choices.

From my own experience, I knew that healthy choices on the body, mind, and spirit levels are essential to total well-being. Being particularly conscious of the impact of sugar and yeast on all aspects of wellness, I'd like to take this opportunity to share some of the lessons I learned...

The Great American Sugar Habit

I've described my own struggle in dealing with sugar addiction. But why is it an addiction?

All the things humans find addictive—drugs, alcohol, gambling, sex, love, motivation, achievement, praise, and sugar!—trigger releases of the neurotransmitter dopamine in the pleasure center of the brain.

Concentrated sugar, like narcotics, can trigger massive dopamine release: CT scans show that the pleasure center of the brain lights up on sugar just the way it does on cocaine. You can't get that level of release from whole, organic foods from natural sources, but you can get it from junk foods, sodas, bottled juices and other sweet drinks, and processed carbs, all basic elements of the mainstream American diet! And so people who are vulnerable to addictive substances are particularly at risk of addiction to sugar and junk food...and as they become more dependent, they need increasing amounts to get the same result: the classic addictive pattern.

When you're consuming refined sugar and fructose, carbs, and junk food in large and increasing quantities, the level of glucose in your bloodstream increases past the point that your body can balance it. You may start to experience symptoms, such as blurred vision, fatigue, frequent hunger and thirst, heavy urination, dry mouth and dry or itchy skin, unexplained weight loss or gain, and recurring infections. Eventually your cells become resistant to insulin, and this can lead to obesity, fatty liver, heart disease, and particularly type II diabetes.

And studies indicate that high sugar consumption doesn't only affect the health of your body—it's been linked to brain fog, moodiness, irritability, anxiety, depression, nervousness, and deficiencies in memory and cognitive health.

The Sugar-Fueled Yeast Feast

When you're consuming a lot of sugar, your blood glucose peaks with every meal or snack—and this leaves you vulnerable to a surge of yeast. For example, a breakfast of sugary cereal, juice, toast, and coffee first thing in the morning when your blood sugar is low, sets up a perfect yeast feast. The caffeine speeds up your heart rate and quickens your pulse, making the sugar surge even faster. Multiply this by the sugar, carbs, and caffeine you eat in each meal or snack, and you've got a systemic yeast problem in the making!

Low estrogen due to the menstrual cycle or menopause, and beauty products and household cleansers containing phthalates, can also boost yeast levels. Estrogen feeds the gut bacterium acidophilus, which helps to keep yeast under control…but menstruation, menopause, and some chemical compounds disrupt the functioning of the hormonal system, reducing natural estrogen levels and leaving you open to yeast surges. You can find information on these endocrine disruptors here: http://www.ewg.org/research/dirty-dozen-list-endocrine-disruptors

Healthy Solutions to the Sugar/Yeast Spiral

As my doctor told me, the first thing to do is to cut the supply of sugar to the yeast overgrowth. Processed sugar and grains are particular troublemakers here. I learned to read labels obsessively and avoid the many variations on sugar, nectar, honey, syrup, cane crystals, dehydrated or concentrated juice, sweetener, fructose, dextrose, sucrose, glucose, lactose, maltose, xylose, dextrin, saccharose, sorghum, molasses, honey, treacle, and turbinado. If an ingredient ends in —ose, it's a sugar!

I began cutting out yeast by avoiding alcohol, breads, pastries and other baked goods, and grain-based snack foods such as crackers and pretzels. For a more complete list and detailed instructions for an elimination diet, I used "The Yeast Connection" as my guidebook.

Most of all, I learned that regaining my health is not all about deprivation! Step-by-step, I re-trained my body to appreciate foods that have vibrancy and give sustained energy instead of rocket fuel:

- Building meals around whole foods—fresh fruits, vegetables, and proteins (whether animal or plant-based).
- Keeping meals balanced. Especially, eating a breakfast that has protein and healthy fat (for example, a green with hemp protein and avocado). This helps to keep hormones and energy steady through the day.

- Avoiding the residue of hormone-disrupting fertilizers and systemic herbicides and pesticides by going the extra step to buy organic, non-GMO foods.
- Taking probiotics and eating fermented foods (for example, yogurt, kefir, kombucha, sauerkraut, kimchi) daily.
- Drinking water steadily throughout the day to flush toxins from your body and improve the performance of every system.

Beyond the level of nutrition, I learned to tend my body and build my energy with movement and sleep.

While yoga works well for me because it helps with my mind/body/spirit balance, any regular movement practice (for example, dancing, jogging, gardening, walking, or hiking) will get blood flow to all the organs, flush out toxins, and boost endorphins to reduce stress, anxiety, and depression and stabilize mood swings.

Sleep helps the body to reduce inflammation, built immune responses, balance hormones, and balance blood glucose (among many other benefits!).

Deeper Healing through Mindfulness Practices

If I've learned one big lesson from my healing journey, it's the importance of mindfulness practices in supporting healing. While a healthy diet dealt with the physical causes of my sugar/yeast imbalance, I discovered that that was just the beginning; I also needed to work on the mind and spirit levels.

I began a practice of daily meditation with cognitive behavioral practices to decrease stress and overwhelm. I began working with a counselor about my anger over not marrying a man I'd dated for six years.

Mindfulness taught me the importance of being in the present moment and not spinning off into imagined scenarios. It also helped to balance my tendency to workaholism: I would overextend myself to keep people from seeing that deep down I didn't feel I was enough. Of course, this only fed my insecurities: *What if I couldn't do everything I'd committed to do? What if I didn't get this done, or I didn't get to this place on time—what would people think of me?*

I realized the importance of pausing to take a deep breath and check in with my inner wisdom before making a decision. I recognized that I needed to be sure that the agreements I made were in alignment with my soul. If I am affirming that I am a healthy, well person, am I making choices that support this affirmation?

These questions rippled out into every aspect of my life—my work, my self-care, my socializing and play. I realized I especially needed to do this in my romantic relationships...especially in choosing my romantic partners!

I recognized I had the power to make healthy choices if I wanted vibrant health and wellness. By consciously choosing positive perceptions over negative judgments and establishing daily practices like "appreciation breaks" throughout the day, I reduced my stress and anger and began to see the beauty in the world and the people around me.

Offering Hope: It Can Be Done!

My journey from massive sugar and yeast imbalance to vibrant wellness didn't take place in one day. It's been a long process, with setbacks and plateaus and sudden surges forward. I've been blessed to have the support of healthcare providers, body-workers, energy healers, family, and friends along the path. There's been no magical one-shot answer!

But I think that's exactly the point: The healing has taken place along the way. Because the root of the sugar/yeast imbalance lay in emotional patterns and eating habits I'd developed in my childhood, it couldn't be solved with one pill or procedure. Those habits had to be unraveled and their effects slowly undone. Along the way I learned about myself and about what I had to offer to the world.

Challenging as it's been, I wouldn't give up one step of that journey. And I am honored and proud to be able to use the lessons I've learned to help others. My mission/passion is to assist others in uprooting the core of their illness/dis-"ease" and teaching them how to heal with nutritional wellness, so they can do what they love with Zest and Harmony. Hence, the name of my company, Zest and Harmony!

Cassandra Herbert — holistic nurse psychotherapist, wellness educator, healthy eating coach, speaker and author — who supports overwhelmed, overextended, tired, worried perfectionist women with shifting from the superwoman syndrome to a woman who nourishes her mind, body and spirit with nutritional wellness for more peace, vibrancy and harmony.

Cassandra believes you are a full and complete person and assists in uprooting the core issues that cause mental blocks and/or illness and dis- ease. She is passionate about assisting you with tapping into your inner wisdom and strength so you can heal.

Her two businesses are Zest and Harmony Counseling/Coaching and Just BEE Wellness. Zest and Harmony provides individual couples and group counseling and couching around nutritional wellness — things that nourish your body, mind and spirit. Just BEE Wellness is an online community, which provides you with resources, from wellness experts around world to inspire and support you on your wellness journey so you can have a balanced, empowered and energized life.

Cassandra's life mission is empowering people on how to advocate for their wellness and what we can do as a society to change the current healthcare system from a culture of sick "care" to one of health and wellness.

Cassandra may be contacted at:
www.zestandharmonycounseling.com
www.justbeewellness.com
https://www.facebook.com/ZestandHarmonyCounseling
https://www.facebook.com/Justbeewellness
Cassandra@zestandharmonycounseling.com
800-463-0362

Creating Sacred Space

Part One: Inspiration

Mindy Wagner

Be who you are! Joseph Campbell wrote *"The privilege of a lifetime is being who you are."*

My focus is to help us do this by creating a conducive environment by also being "Where You Are."

By opening the door to an alignment with our true selves we are greatly nourished by starting from where you are and making it Sacred. There are many souls on a conscious path to enlightenment, but it has been my experience that not so many realize the importance of living in a way of beauty, order, and intention in their actual living and working places. Not so many have placed an importance on daily rituals and practices that help us interweave the health of our own bodies, minds, and spirits with our home, our garden, our desk, our bed, our kitchen, etc.

What is creating Sacred Space other than our desire to reconnect with source? Our divine intelligence, the home of all the laws of nature resides within our true selves. Learning how to create an interior and exterior that puts a shape on our deepest longings, fosters our visions and reclaims the genius of our individuality gives us the platforms where our body, mind, and spirit can rest easy, where we cook our meals, and cleanse ourselves of the day's debris, and where we meditate and rest. We capture this holy energy when we bow before Sacred Space.

As your body is a temple, so is your home. No matter if you live in one small room in a shared apartment or house, or a grand and luxurious villa. Your home is a living thing and must be treated that way.

We may have experienced, while traveling on vacation, an awe-inspiring hotel entrance with its marble pillars, exuberantly flowing fountains, and gracious seating to welcome us to someplace special. There is a carved table resplendent with gorgeous flowers as we enter the lobby, a fragrant scent in the air, music playing, and our hearts leap! Something awakens in us as we enter a grand space like that. Can we imagine finding a feeling like that when we enter our home or workplace?

When you have created your Sacred Space you will find that no matter what is happening in your life, you can go there and re-find your center, your inner quiet. And hear the voice of your Higher Self.

We exchange energy and communicate with everything in our environment. Part of wholeness and wellness is creating a home inside ourselves so that we are "home" anywhere we go. The world is our family...you recognize yourself in everyone no matter how outwardly different they may appear to be. That inner knowing is derived from a number of angles. One angle that may be underrated is how we live in that place we call our "house." Just as a turtle carries her shell on her back everywhere she goes, we carry the energy of our home everywhere we go.

Literally...the house we live in is an expression of our inner state of being. The routines we create, our daily rituals are spokes in the wheel that moves us into raising our daily life to the level of the Sacred.

Everyone needs a sanctuary, a place to find peace and anchor the spirit in the body, align the whirling chakras. Everyone needs a safe place. It may be a small room or an entire home. It may be your office or studio, your garden...it needs to be somewhere.

The Art of Feng-Shui

Feng means wind, and **Shui** means water. The movement of air creates wind and also moves the ocean and all the bodies of water on the planet. Without air we cannot breathe—we will die. Without water we will eventually die.

We ourselves are Feng-Shui incarnate. All that comprises the elements are present within our bodies, minds, and spirits. All is always on the move! Nothing in our bodies stops. It is stagnation in our bodies, toxins, and blockages that create disease and death .

Feng-Shui teaches that the earth, our land, water and air, our buildings, homes, rooms, and furnishings are also considered bodies, and together we live in a reciprocal relationship. We give to our land and home; our land and home gives to us like the center; the Tai-Chi rotates Yin and Yang in a constant spiral motion.

The goal of using Feng-Shui techniques is to raise the Chi or energy in both systems—in our bodies stimulated by our home's energy and our general environment; and from our electromagnetic fields and intentions of the mind and heart which we emanate in concert with our environment.

Feng-Shui started as a land-art in China roughly 5,000 years ago. It was cognized by the great seers who planned cities and towns for the best quality of life. Using the art of observation and connecting art and science, the geomancers of that time looked at the juxtaposition of mountains and hills to bodies of water and fertile lands to farm. Signs and symbols, plants and animals, and the natural elements of fire, earth, metal, water, and wood are intrinsic forces driving Feng-Shui.

The powers of Yin and Yang are basic to understanding any space. Yin and Yang are the contrasts, the opposites that flow back and forth into one another. Light and dark, dry and wet, bold and retreating, masculine and feminine are examples of Yin and Yang. The Feng-Shui practitioner looks at any space, be it the land or the building, the interior and exterior, through the enlightened lens of the sage. We call it seeing through Feng- Shui eyes.

As an Interior Designer I have learned first to design the space with freedom and creativity, allowing my intuitive and creative flow to inspire me. Once the space has been articulated in my design, I can then go back and review it using the layout of the Feng-Shui Ba-Gua, or sacred energy blueprint, and then I can see what changes need to be made.

The Ba-Gua is the octagonal form developed to give meaning to the nine areas on the map of the home and land. These Guas, or sectors, each have their own energy vortex. There are eight Guas plus the Tai-Chi area in the center of any space. The Guas are known as:

1. Career or The Journey, Fame, and Reputation
2. Helpful Friends and Travel
3. Prosperity
4. Mountain (or Wisdom and Learning)
5. Love and Partnership
6. Family
7. Health and Elders
8. Creativity and Children
9. In the center, the 9th area is known as the Tai-Chi and also drives Health.

As the poet said: *"A thing of beauty is a Joy Forever"*

The Journey

We all have a life story that begins in the womb. As we become awake in our new body when we are babies, our chapters are being written. My life story illustrates that one's destiny and purpose will find you along the way. I honestly feel that my life found me...and I embraced her!

Becoming a designer of interiors and infusing my projects with a sense of well-being and liveliness has become my signature. Fusing together several aspects of my passions and interests—aspects that I kept separate from one another for decades—as our culture became more accepting, has now become exactly who I am—whole, perfect, and complete.

Before I went to school to be an Interior Designer and while I was in college as a student of fine art and art history, I became a devotee of Transcendental Meditation. My daily practice of meditation, yoga, and Ayurveda was a deep, personal commitment and way of life. As a budding professional Interior Designer working in a materialistic and glamorous industry, I kept my spiritual practices to myself.

But twenty years hence from the start of my career, it came to light in the media that Westerners in the building and design field were embracing the ancient art of Feng-Shui. And before too long there was much talk and education about its parent, from the Vedic teachings of India, called Vastu. Each of these Asian arts was the answer to my duality in life, as they brought together spirituality with the design of our dwellings. The restoration of these enlightened arts brought to us by the sages of China and India have given a new flame to the candle that lights my practices. Creating a sanctuary—and knowing how to meditate in it and how to work with prayer and intention—has made each day holy and a joy.

Your Destiny Will Find you

My very first sanctuary was under the dining room table in our apartment in Queens, New York. As a young child I could curl up and fit easily under the dining-room table. The tabletop was my roof; its legs were the stable confines of my first art studio, the humble beginnings of a lifelong pastime of drawing on paper. Under that table I was safe and had my private enclave where the yelling and anger in the household faded from my senses. The stress and strife of our little dwelling in a 900-square-foot apartment fell away under that table.

My paper was the clean side of stapled mimeograph paper that my father supplied me with, left over from his Thursday night volunteering at the credit union. Many children like to draw and paint. I took to it like a refugee from the storm. My parents noticed that I had the natural ability of an artist...I drew everything I could think of. It was natural and an occupation that induced a place within me that felt like shelter. It was not often a happy home, but the world inside me was a rainbow.

Although my father wanted me to become a secretary...a message he related loud and clear...I never wavered in my resolve to go to art school. In senior year of high school, we could choose an "major", and I jumped at the chance to be in art classes with like-minded students.

The environment I grew up in as a child did not herald my eventual profession. If what you see is what you know, then it was not a likely path for me. My mother's decor was to match the color scheme of our parakeet, Twinkie. Our furniture in my early years was handed down to us from my Russian grandmother...mahogany brown, brown carpet, brown sofa. But, in later years when my mother returned to the workforce, her earnings went towards some new furnishings, all turquoise. It matched our parakeet! If I never see turquoise shag carpet again, it will be too soon!

High school days fell in the year of the flower children, the hippie revolution. The concept of Interior Designer was foreign to my vocabulary. But "Artist" was my holy grail. It was a creative time when the norm was being sent adrift. Think: Abstract Expressionism, Andy Warhol, The Beatles Sargent Pepper, Mod Clothing, and Haight Ashbury.

Our art teacher gave us a special homework assignment...to go to the museums and write a report. That museum trip was my first journey to the Sacred, the emergence of my holy grail.

I didn't know what an Interior Designer was until I was about to become one. But when that door opened, I recognized the right career fit, and I embraced the education and the training at the college level.

Up until the moment when I discovered the field of Interior Design as a career path, I was stuck in the idea of being an artist in the way I had seen it...the painter, the sculptor, working in traditional modes of paint on canvas; pencil on paper. However, out of need, *"Destiny called!"*

I think we can agree that life is a journey and we are on it! I believe that our story is already written ...we just have to open the chapters. Looking back, hindsight reveals how my journey has been pushed and prompted by some unseen guidance...or how else would I have arrived in such a place of beauty and spiritual well-being?

It is also true that we must agree to the adventure...and seize the opportunities—the open doors that keep appearing along the way. There were platforms that I wanted to stand on, and I felt a burning desire to see those platforms appear ...and so when suddenly someone would say *"I'm going here,"* I'd say, *"Take me with you!"* And they would. And that is how a few of my highest callings were met.

We must believe in our dreams, ask for them to come true, and be alert when that moment comes...sometimes cloaked in-dress that we would never have expected.

Growing up in a small apartment with a family who felt held-back by lack of income, no car, disappointments , health problems, anger, and resentment, a child like me who was so naturally creative and over-flowing with joy and expression, that child is challenged to stay open. But just as the green grass grows through the concrete pavement, the creative soul finds her way through.

Living in an atmosphere often charged with negativity and even fear, I developed the armor of keeping my dreams in their own Sacred Place Without much support or interest from family, I was lucky to have a few teachers who brought out my inherent talents.

The chance to be the artist creating set designs for our sixth grade production of "Snow White" was the first artistic opportunity that set me on this path. I painted a large castle wall rendered in stone and some stately trees with poster paint on brown paper glued to cardboard. The set remained on stage for the whole production, in which I also acted and sang the role of the Mean Queen.

My mother gifted me in childhood with ballet lessons and piano lessons...she was happy that I left her alone when I spent hours drawing pictures on those reams of used paper my dad gave me. I was not without some gifts and encouragement from my family. On a good day, my parents sang together. My mother played piano, and they both had beautiful voices. My parents even sang along with the popular singers on television...Frank Sinatra; Sammy Davis, Jr.; Connie Francis; and so many others.

My brother played guitar, and he and I sang folk songs together. This love of music and entertainment was what I knew of The Arts. My mother, who had been an actress in her younger days, managed to take us to Broadway shows. Theatre is also for me a Sacred Place. The metaphor, originally written by Shakespeare and paraphrased here, is that *"Life is a stage and we are the actors upon it."*

My first Sacred Space appeared to me as a result of the assignment my high school art teacher gave us in our senior year. There were two trips that I made and made solo...first to The Museum of Modern Art and next to The Metropolitan Museum of Art in New York City.

I believe that we were written to script to our lives. It was a nice touch that I was born into a New York City family. In New York one could travel by bus and subway or walk city blocks to the great museums, galleries, and edifices of the world. I believe that my soul planned it that way.

Once I took that first bus ride to the subway station and that first walk from the subway, just a few blocks to The Museum of Modern Art, I was free. I was free to open the next door to my life. The MOMA was just the start for me. The ritual of traveling into Manhattan from Queens was like leaving the hut for the palace. My first stop was the museum's cafeteria for all I could afford—the ritual l of coffee and a corn muffin. It was usually raining outside on my museum pilgrimages, for some reason, which made the light, color, and warmth of the museum a sanctuary.

But, it was the European Collection at The Met that pulled me in! The Museum itself is a quintessential Sacred Space. It welcomes all architecturally as it sits high atop its granite steps, looking like a Greco/Roman temple. Inside is a great Rotunda...gathering the great, important, and sacred energies to bring together the people and cultures of the world, circulating the Chi or energy, and what in Vastu is called the Brahmastan.

My first visit there directed by my high school teacher was by myself, as if on a pilgrimage. My instinct was to head to the left, past the Egyptian, Greek, and Roman rooms and into the European collection.

Before me was a gigantic oil-on-board or canvas with an ornate frame... the artist may have been Spanish or from the Netherlands...and I came face-to-face with the deep and lush image of St. Francis in the Garden.

So moved by the great painting, I stood transfixed, entering into it... never before had any image reached into my soul. Being with this great piece of art and feeling so many emotions, I was transformed and felt some inner agreement and dedication to a life that would include both art forms and spirituality.

The Journey Home

It was in Northern California that I was called home. After the first year of college, starting my art classes in the second year, my social life and a natural desire to be independent led me away from home. I was not performing well in school, save that of my art classes. I was young and found myself in an abusive relationship with a young man who caused me to feel great shame and hurt. I dropped out of school to support him at the age of 19, and he cheated on me. I went back to live with my parents. An opportunity to escape what felt like my failed existence in my hometown of New York City presented itself. *"Destiny called again!"*

I was invited to visit my dear friends who had left New York for Southern California to play in their rock band at a Laguna Beach nightclub. They extended an open invitation to a few of their friends, and I found a way to go.

The glorious West Coast, the rocky Pacific Ocean beaches, and my fun loving friends awaited me on a grand adventure. The very air of California lifted me, opened me, and scared me to death! An adventure swimming in a sea cave with my best buddy, Beth, clinging to the rocks as the tides came in, nearly caused me to drown as I was paralyzed by my own fear. As the rising waves hit the boulders we were swimming around, studying beautiful tide pools and iridescent sea anemones, the power of the waves that came crashing into the cave overwhelmed me. Beth had to slap me to get me to swim out of there.

Mother Nature was our great attraction in California. As the weeks slipped by and I became a "Californian", another friend, Mary, who was Native American by descent, agreed that I could ride along with her and her two dogs, Buffalo and Spirit, in her old Chevy up the coast. Between us we had little money, but we had our backpacks, her car, a Coleman stove, one mummy sleeping bag, and two large, warm dogs. We traveled up the scenic Pacific Coast Highway for two months, sleeping in campgrounds, finding water to swim in, meeting people who caused us no harm. It was sleeping under the stars and embracing the breathtaking mountains perched above the great ocean, talking to the trees, and inhaling the fragrance of eucalyptus that healed my soul.

By the time we reached Lake Tahoe and then The Russian River further north, Mary was ready to go. She dropped me off south of Santa Cruz in the Santa Cruz Mountains, the home of The Redwood forest, by the ocean. There I stayed with a loosely organized group of hippie friends. Our goal was absolutely nothing! Day-to-day. Sun-up, sun-down. Some days we played music, other days went to the beach. One day, we went to Hearst Castle and worked for a few cents an hour matching threads to tapestries that were being repaired by restorers. Life had a meaningful and meaningless rhythm.

We don't always know how we will be healed or by whom. Or what may call to us when we are ready to hear. One night my calling arrived with no appointment. My band of friends was going camping in Swanton in the Redwood forest.

The giant redwood trees, thousands of years old, stand in thick groves. The base of the larger trees forms a house big enough to enter for shelter. They soar straight and high like natural skyscrapers of nature. The smell of the redwood and the pine needles forms a soft carpet and creates a fragrant and magical atmosphere deep in the forest. One feels the primeval energies of earth, wood, and sky. A knowing that there is something greater than our limited selves is unmistakable. The sacred sound of the wind through the trees takes one's soul beyond the place of standing.

The sound called to me as the sun was setting on a late August night. My friends were gathering kindling for a campfire as the rays of the sun cascaded through the trees in great shafts of light. I walked away from the group, alone, led by instinct to a circle of great redwood giants, forming a bowl effect. They appeared to me as a Cathedral of The Trees, the columns of light like the great sword of the Archangel Michael. I stood before the shafts of light, living beings in their own right. They spoke to me that God was here to meet me. I felt the Holy presence. Reaching deeply into my heart, tears running down my cheeks, I had my first true inner knowing, being whole for a moment in the Sacred Space. I became it, and it became me.

Within minutes I walked away from the timelessness of that moment and found my friend David who had the car we arrived in. It was about 8:30 p.m. I asked him to take me to The San Francisco Airport so that I could fly standby back to New York. With me, I had my backpack, a guitar, a return trip ticket, and a few dollars. David was baffled, but in those days we went with the flow.

Arriving at the airport, which was at least an hour away, I was able to catch the red-eye to La Guardia airport. I found myself in Queens, New York, in the grimy airport at 6:00 a.m. in the morning. I was wearing shoes, a peasant blouse and skirt, with a dirty backpack, and a eucalyptus necklace. I wasn't sure what the cab driver was thinking as he took me to my best friend's house. *Just another hippie teenager going home to Mom?* My wild self was discovered, and a mission for my life was born to recapture sacredness everywhere I walked on the path of this life.

When the Student is Ready...

That wise saying: *"When the student is ready, the teacher will appear,"* was true for me. Following my epiphany in the Redwood Forest of California, I re-entered college , a commuter college, and went back to live in the apartment with my parents.

My inner world had changed; my resolve was anchored to find a path, a spiritual path. Isolating myself socially from the old crowd as much as possible, I concentrated on my courses. Thirsty for knowledge about how to get on a path for my life I read every book about meditation, healing, and esoteric, metaphysical knowledge that I could find. My older brother, now a librarian, offered suggestions for books to read, including Baba Ram Dass's "Be Here Now." That book gave me the courage to dig deep into myself that there would be a community for me, somehow.

The moment came as I studied quietly, alone at a table by the window in the student union of Queens College. My friend, Anne, walked up to me to say hello. She looked different. Her eyes were brighter; she radiated happiness and confidence. She mentioned that she had stopped smoking cigarettes with the help of doing Transcendental Meditation, as taught by Maharishi Mahesh Yogi. But it was more than that.

TM, as she called it, was a path to enlightenment. Anne invited me to join her for an evening in Manhattan at the famous Town Hall Concert Hall for a night in mid- March when His Holiness, Maharishi, would be speaking. Maha means great, and Rishi means seer. I was in for a treat, as the term "great seer" was just a small taste of what this would mean to me. The attendees would be those who were already initiated into TM, but Anne felt that I could pass for one!

That night, the March winds were whipping around the corridors of the chilly Manhattan streets. We were lined up with hundreds of other people for more than an hour, clutching hot coffee and chocolate drinks in

Styrofoam cups. There was celebration in the air, chapped cheeks, and sparkling spirits of excitement, as only an enlightened being can herald the advance of his appearance.

Once seated in the old red velvet seats of Town Hall, a refined gentleman in a suit stood center stage and asked us to close our eyes and meditate before Maharishi would come out to speak. I closed my eyes, barely containing the energy that I felt. I made myself small in the seat, and although I was not yet a TM meditator, I felt the inner presence.

Like a breeze rolling in from the ocean on a summer morning, the gentleness and the pure joy of a wave of bliss opened my eyes, and there he was! Almost floating, he walked with effortless grace in his white dhoti and brown leather sandals to be seated on a white sofa surrounded by hundreds of flowers and a large framed portrait of his teachers, Guru Dev behind him. Quietly he said, *Jai Guru Dev,*" a salutation of great love and respect for his teacher and the Holy Tradition that preceded his time on earth to the roots of human beginnings.

I was home. Home at last, seated in that red chair among hundreds of others. It was done. I was here, and I would be on this path to learn and to be at one with this great joy.

My initiation to TM took place the following month. The first time I had seen an altar was on the day of my learning. The instruction took place in a small room, the teacher reciting a Puja ceremony before this altar of incense, rice, camphor, candles, flowers, fruit, and a picture of Guru Dev.

The holiness in the room was real and true, as my instructor sang the ancient Vedic Puja, a ceremony of gratitude, calling in the sages of this tradition to be present for my learning. My new mantra was absorbed within me, becoming a part of me for life. Now I had a technique and a path.

SOLITIUDE

"Poem from Skowhegan, Maine" by Mindy Wagner

Fallen to lilacs
All the winds blowing around on an almost full moon
Papers fly up from taped wall places
Lilac breeze rushes
Now I sleep and wait the day of the fortune teller
Teller of fortunes your breath has sent me to lilacs.

© 2014 by Mindy S. Wagner

I was trudging up the snowy muddy hill in my L.L. Bean parka...on my way home from my new job as a credit manager at the JCPENNY on the outskirts of Skowhegan, Maine. The road led to Canada. For a girl who couldn't pass math class, an artist, my job taking credit applications was the perfect misfit. With no car, the one-mile uphill trek to my one-and- a-half room bungalow atop the hillside of the Malbon farm was a fitting metaphor for swimming upstream. I was 25 years old and had come back to Skowhegan for a misguided and failed attempt at romance. Now I was alone and broke, not to mention brokenhearted. Every day as I clumped up the icy dreary road, I imagined that I was a soldier in the Israeli army—"if she could do it, then I could do it"—survive.

The bungalow was built as a temporary shelter for Mr. and Mrs. Malbon, now 80 years old. While they built their lovely farmhouse, they lived in the bungalow. She was now widowed and welcomed my renting the sparse dwelling. It had a hot plate, a sink, a bathroom, and a small bedroom and cupboard for clothes. There was room for a chair outside the bedroom. No television, and it had a radio with three scratchy stations.

As I thought myself to be a landscape painter, I had little else to do except look out the window and draw the bare black trees against the snowy hills.

When spring came to Skowhegan, the ground thawed and by summer I said goodbye to the moose on the roadside, the broken bicycle I was riding on the hill, and the empty room. I said goodbye to Mrs. Malbon, and all the loneliness that launched me to my next chapter.

Food Among the Flowers

One year later: Mrs. Gray was a grand dame of interior design and head of the Interior Design Department at Palm Beach Community College. She was my teacher and led our group of students on a field trip to The Miami Design district. We were first-year students, *newbies*, and our eyes and hands were alive with wonder at the luxury of silk and linen, tapestry and velvet, in the small showrooms that wove in and out of the old streets of Little Havana.

Mrs. Gray, who wore heels and a gray linen suit in the heat of Miami, planned our day in the elegance of the showrooms, and at noon we had reservations for the whole class to have lunch at a small and special restaurant on a corner street in the design district. As we fell into "Food Among the Flowers," I gasped. It was circular and all the walls were mirrored. There was a leather upholstered banquette for seating, which went all around like a horseshoe, and on the ledges above the seatbacks below the mirrors were live lush tropical flowers. The flowers, vines, and leaves were doubled by their reflections in the mirrors...and the feeling was that of being deep in a jungle paradise, a magical grotto.

It was there that I knew I had been called to my life, alone no more, lost no more...but dropped into such delight to find my way...and give other people this gift of divine and precious space, as beautiful and surprising as food among the flowers.

Sanctuary

How do we make Sacred Space? There is a practical approach which we combine with a spiritual feeling and intention. My first seminar on Feng-Shui was at the Smithsonian Institute taught by Feng -Shui master, William Spears. William's opening statement at the seminar was that for Americans, the greatest Feng-Shui tool is a box of Hefty Trash bags! Everyone laughed. How true that is…we Americans are always buying things, accumulating things, and filling up our rooms and closets with far too much.

Clutter holds back the flow of good energy. Clutter is known as Sha-Chi..or negative chi. How much easier life would be if we didn't have to manage stacks of paper, overstuffed drawers, clothing we never wear, but just push aside…how much cleaner!

The idea that *"Cleanliness is next to Godliness"* rings true for making Sacred Space.

------◆◆◆------

Mindy Wagner established her interior design practice, Mindy Wagner Interior Design, LLC, in 1983. Feng-Shui, she soon discovered, was the missing link between her business life of art and design and her personal practice of meditation, yoga, and dance. Mindy began integrating Feng-Shui and The Art of Sacred Space into her design projects in 1995 and today holds a certification in Feng Shui for Real Estate. Mindy can be contacted for consultations and projects at 240-620-2301 or www.mindywagner.com.

In Alignment With Who You Are

Dixie Bennett

Who knew that vulnerability is the greatest power?

Each and every step along the way of your journey, no matter how shaky, unbalanced, or uncertain: You are whole, perfect, and complete. Right from the day that you were born, until this very moment, has been in perfect design and is in alignment with who you are. Perhaps you don't see it this way, but it is in fact the truth. It is how you perceive the experience and the expectations you set around it. Each experience offers a gift. Are you wondering how can there be a gift in your experience? Let me show you; are you ready to find the gift?

I would like to share a dream I had recently. This dream was surprising to me because it involved someone who most definitely was not a soul mate in a romantic definition. It began in darkness—mostly gray, black, and white. I was with my ex in the trailer that we lived in. We also worked together. All our co-workers adored him. I found myself yelling inside my head, *"Why can't you see him for who he is?"* I was filled with silent anger and rage. The company fired me, and I was extremely angry. *"Why is everyone so blind? Why don't they fire him?"* Yet, he just went about his business and ignored my anger. He then asked me if I would like to go for a drive in the country and, with the logic of dreams, I agreed.

As we drove my dream changed into vibrant, lively colors complete with beautiful foliage and a dancing creek. Peaceful. We soon arrived at a ranch in the middle of nowhere. There weren't any roads, but there was a hustle and bustle of activity from children, men and women of all ages, including the elderly. When we arrived they were all very happy to see him. I still couldn't figure this out: *"Why couldn't anyone see him for who he was?"* Suddenly an old woman said to me, *"Dear, you must be so lucky to have a man like him; he is a godsend."*

We both looked over at him as he busied himself with mending odds-and-ends. This was strange to me because I didn't know him as a fix-it kind of guy. Suddenly a woman broke into the room and announced that she was looking for a Bowen and Craniosacral Therapist. Without hesitation I spoke up, *"That's me; that is what I am."*

She said, *"Let's not waste time; we have to go now!"* So off I went and climbed into her Jeep without a thought. We drove deeper into the countryside where we came upon a retreat center. When we walked in, there were six massage tables lined up with people on them waiting to receive treatment. There were hundreds of thousands of people lined out the door waiting for their turn.

I woke up and realized the gift of that relationship! Without that experience years ago I would not be who I am now, nor would I have gone through the deep healings that I have experienced in order to realize my learnings and reclaim the pieces of my shattered self.

Beginning the Journey

I want you to know how magnificent healing can be; it can come from the most powerful and unexpected situations. When I was 19, I met my now ex, who I later found out had a rap sheet so long that the police were shocked and asked me what I was doing with this guy. He did all the right things to rope me in. It was a textbook case of an abusive relationship. I want to focus on how I got out and used this experience to realize my gifts and deepen my insights.

We were introduced through mutual friends. He was strong, attentive, exciting—tall, dark, and handsome. He was mysterious, well-groomed, impressive, always showed up at exactly the right time; he always knew what to say. He made me feel special and important; he took me dancing, and I felt protected. We quickly moved in together. Then something changed, he started to grow distant.

Slowly and over time, I found myself being herded, guided into a cage. I slowly became alienated from friends and family. I became unhappy, nervous, filled with worry, unloved, and alone. He started to become more and more moody. He claimed my car as his, and started to come and go as he pleased. Then he started sitting in on my shifts at the restaurant, watching my every move and interaction.

I assumed when he left during the day that he was going to a job, but I never really was sure where he went. I didn't know any of his family or friends. When the bills came due, we barely had enough. I took on another job to make ends meet, and I started working all the time—shift work serving at a local restaurant and an industrial job in the evening working until midnight. The more I worked, the less I saw of him.

I have to admit I had no idea about the man I was living with. There was a lot of secrecy, darkness, and pain around this relationship. I lost my voice, my strength, my courage, my identity, and my dignity. I was sad and alone, unwanted, with no one in my corner.

He suddenly started to disappear for days at a time. When he came back, he offered no explanations—only to do it again a few days later. I will never forget the time I came home early from a shift. He had just been there, and I could still see the wet footprints on the carpet leading from the shower to the bedroom. It felt like he was still in the house, but he was nowhere to be found. How could he come and go like that without as much as a note? I was crushed.

One day he came to my work, just as I finished my shift. He drove up to me and told me to get in. I obeyed. He started to drive out of town onto a back-country road. I suddenly felt sick to my stomach. I looked at him, and he was crying, drunk, and still drinking whiskey. Why hadn't I noticed that before I got into the car? He was driving fast, swerving all over the road and gave every indication that he didn't care if he or I lived or died. All I could do was keep calm, and I asked God for guidance. He was hysterical and not making any sense at all. All I remember was trying to keep him on the road and to keep him focused.

The Courage to Leap

I finally talked him into driving back to town. I was so frightened—no, I was beyond frightened. When we came back to town I was grateful, and for a brief moment I thought I'd repeat the past and try to ignore his behavior, but I knew in my heart if I didn't leave now, I would regret it. He wasn't physically abusive with me, but he was a master at head games, and I felt it was only a matter of time before things escalated to physical violence.

He then disappeared again. I decided it was now or never. It was September, the middle of a busy harvest, when I called my farming parents to come and help me move. If they didn't come now, I wouldn't have the courage to try later at a more convenient time—there is *never a more convenient time*. I had found the courage and the support I needed when my parents showed up. I was ready to go, and I was determined for it to be on my terms. Unfortunately, he came back with a vengeance and resumed stalking me.

I finally understood that he had stalked me from the very beginning. Again, this silent predator would show up seconds behind me, wherever I was. That's when my mom and I went to the police to get a restraining order. On the desk they had his file that looked about a foot high. The officer asked, *"What are you doing with this guy?"*

Unfortunately, no crime had been committed, and we were on our own. The story doesn't end there, however. I have realized over the years that I am grateful for this experience and what I chose to be part of because of the knowledge I gained. It seems I needed a big lesson for me to realize I have the power to direct my own life. I had it all along, but for some reason I gave it away. Even while I was in the depths of a miserable situation, I provided for myself. I was resourceful and resilient. I've always had this deep drive and determination to keep going, no matter what.

The gift I found was my courage to walk away and never go back. When I decided to leap, the universe provided me with all the resources and assistance I needed to make it happen. I found my inner strength. I listened to my inner guidance and heard that voice that said, *"It's time to go."*

That voice has come through for me many times. When it speaks, I listen without judgment, and it never steers me wrong. I trust, therefore I am supported.

Confidence and Balance

Years later I was tested again. I will never forget October 2004. I had decided to take a spontaneous day-off from work, a "me" day for the first time ever in my life. I felt I needed to do some deep thinking and get out of the city. I needed something radical to break out of the corporate mold. I needed to get out and take a break from everything.

I hated my job; life was hard; and it seemed to get harder every day. I was in a funk, depressed, and wondering what my life really had to offer. Little did I know that this day would be the catalyst to cracking me open and setting me forth onto the path of enlightenment with the realization that I am in alignment with who I am in every moment, of every day.

I had no idea where I was going to go on this spontaneous "me" day until that morning. For some reason I was drawn to Grassi Lakes in Canmore, Alberta, Canada, a place I had never been and didn't know much about. Some would say I was divinely guided. I had no idea what the phrase meant at the time, but I was guided intuitively, whether I was consciously aware of it or not.

When I arrived it was gently snowing and beautiful. I decided to take the easier trail to the right that meandered through dense forest. I had forgotten that weather in the mountains could be quite different from the city. The higher I climbed; the more ice mounds I encountered. I went as far as I could before the ice became impassable for me. I had no problem on the way up; however, it became apparent that I wasn't properly equipped for the descent. I carefully negotiated the ice mounds and was managing, until suddenly I lost my footing. I went into an uncontrolled slide and hurtled right to the edge of the cliff where a tiny, bent tree somehow stopped my momentum. *How could this be?*

I looked down below me and saw two ice climbers coming up the face of the mountain. I had almost sailed right over them and off the mountain, along with my gloves and walking stick. Lucky for me I still had my keys in my pocket. Where the rock climbers had ropes, pitons, and experience, I had only my fingernails and self-determination to climb to safety.

I slowly made my way up the ice and found a place to just lie still and breathe, staring up at the open sky as snowflakes gently floated down and landed on me, while I appreciated life. The air was clean and clear. Not a sound. Time stopped. I was shaking, but I knew I was alive. I believe God put that tree there. I believed in that moment that I wasn't ready to die yet. I realized I still had plenty to do, and that I had a bigger purpose even if I still didn't know what that purpose looked like. As I lay there I heard the words come to me: *"Confidence and Balance."* I repeated them to myself out loud all the way back to my car. The phrase gave me peace and has become my personal mantra that I still repeat to this day for grounding, and as a reminder of my strength.

Forgiveness

The truth I discovered about forgiveness is that we have decided to carry the burden of the wrong-doing. The freedom is found when you put down the burden and forgive yourself for carrying it in the first place. What purpose is it giving you other than a reminder of pain?

I had a powerful experience in 2005, shortly after my condo building burned down and I was living in a hotel. It was a new beginning for me: I got to live in a hotel for five months. How many people get to live in a hotel? Believe it or not, I really enjoyed it. I had nothing but a suitcase and two weeks' worth of clothing, but it was a reminder to me that stuff is stuff, and we really can't take it all with us. This period was also a gift because I got to fully experience the pure release of forgiveness.

Through my healing journey, I have found that I have always healed and processed through imagery. One morning I woke in the hotel yelling out loud, *"I forgive you; I forgive you; I forgive you."*

This was upon awakening from another dream where my ex had visited me. He wanted to talk, and I was ignoring him. I had nothing to say to him so he worked around me and became friends with my co-workers and roommates. He was everywhere, and I was angry. I stormed out of the house only to find him following me; he wanted to talk and I kept saying, *"No."* Finally he chased me down and made me look at him. As I did so, I realized I was holding onto anger. He was telling me to let go. I forgave myself for carrying that burden and then I forgave him. I didn't want to carry that heavy bag anymore.

Trust

Another day I will never forget was in July 2006. I had a great deal of chest pain. I couldn't breathe and with every exhalation it became harder to take-in air. It felt like a boa constrictor had wrapped itself around my chest, crushing me, keeping me from breathing in life. It felt like my life force was being taken from me, and I couldn't bring it back. My ribs felt broken; my lungs crushed. The pain was intense and uncomfortable: I tried to sit and it hurt; I tried to lie down on my bed and it hurt; I wanted to cry but nothing came but more pain. Panic was setting in, and I asked myself, *"Is this it; am I dying?"*

It was about 10:00 p.m. at night when I called a friend to take me to the hospital. When we arrived, the nurses put me on the waiting list; they didn't seem too concerned, but kept asking how I was doing and would intermittently take my blood pressure. They didn't say too much, and I didn't seem to be a priority. I secretly found peace in that—I thought maybe it meant that I was okay.

It was a big night in our city as it was opening night for the Calgary Stampede. The hospital was full of chaos with all kinds of injuries that looked more serious than mine. We waited for three hours, which to me felt like eternity. I sat in silence, hoping that all would be fine, as I watched the chaos around me. I found that I retreated inward; I found peace there. And yet again I asked, *"Is this it; am I dying?"* Only silence answered.

I'm pretty stubborn and do not give in easily. I was not giving in to this pain either. I really didn't know what was going on in my body, but I knew it wasn't good. I sat in silence again, just focusing on my breathing, in and out. The struggle seemed to lessen, and I questioned myself. As you know, we can start talking ourselves into believing everything is okay and telling ourselves anything to get out of an emergency waiting room. But this voice inside me said, *"NO, you can't go home."* Little did I know at this time that my will to live was so strong that my body was in fight-mode to save my life. Everything became surreal around me as the pain took over.

Finally, they called my name, and I was able to see a doctor. Once the doctor looked at my file he knew immediately what was wrong. He thought I had pulmonary embolism (blood clots), but ordered a CT scan to be sure. Now that he seemed to know what was going on and took control, I felt safe and fully surrendered to the pain; I was no longer in control. I felt groggy, exhausted, and heavy. I was in and out of consciousness. I asked myself yet again, *"Is this it; am I dying?"*

In my dream state, I saw myself standing at a door. As I stood there, I felt frozen; I couldn't move on. I told myself, *"This can't be it; there is so much more to do; I haven't yet fulfilled my great purpose. I don't yet know what that purpose is, but I know it's big; I know I'm not finished yet; this can't be it; I'm not ready yet."*

I was rushed for a CT scan, where the medical staff put in an IV and pressed fluid into me. I felt it rush through every part of my body from head to toe. It was the strangest sensation. Yet again, I felt I had no control. When the results came back, the doctors informed me that my left leg was filled right to my hip with blood clots. Clots had broken off into little pieces and were filling my lungs, causing me to suffocate almost to death. The doctors and nurses shared how serious this was many times, and they were in awe that I was still alive. I later found out from another source that three women had died in the waiting room earlier that year, with exactly the same symptoms that I exhibited.

I was then bed-ridden for ten days in the hospital. I hated every minute of it. I was very angry. *"Why me?! Why was this happening to me?"* I had no energy; I slept most of the time and remained in silence. I felt so humiliated because I couldn't even get up to use the bathroom. I even tried to sneak out of bed when I thought the nurses weren't watching, only to collapse on the floor. I was not ready to receive assistance from anyone, and my body would not cooperate with me.

The second night I found that the anger consumed me; it overtook my body. I couldn't breathe, and once more I felt like I was drowning. I had to hit the nurses' call button. It felt like they took forever to come. I went into a panic attack; my body started to shake and convulse; I couldn't breathe! When the nurses finally arrived, it took four of them to calm me down.

After that, all I could do was sleep. I was too exhausted to care, and silence was a welcome companion. I tried every night to watch the Stampede fireworks since I had a great window view, but never managed it. I had to learn to walk again. I had little air capacity and thus minimal oxygen for any activity. This created a domino effect that left me incapacitated and unable to walk. I had to retrain my lungs to take-in air so that my body could move.

My goals became small and immediate. First, I wanted to have a shower. It took me a while to get moving and make it there. It took focus just to keep shuffling the few feet to the bathroom. I remember being so tired I couldn't even step into the shower. I shuffled back to bed and tried again the next day. When I managed to actually shower, it took everything I had to get back to the hospital bed where I slept the rest of the day. It was crazy to think how delicate I was. Each day I had a goal to try a little more, and a little more.

When I finally went home, I was off work for another month. Each day I got into my car and drove to a city conservation area—Glenmore Park. The water of the reservoir was soothing to watch. I didn't get out of the car at first. Sometimes I just drove there and sat, and I took a nap because it was so much work just to get there. I made it my goal to go to the park and walk a little further each day. My plan was to keep focusing on my next goal. I showed up every day and kept passing my goals. It gave me hope and strength to realize how far I had come in my rehabilitation. Perseverance and determination, plus my mantra: *"Confidence and Balance"* helped me to heal.

Finding Alternate Healing

The rebuilding I required from the blood clots led me to Craniosacral Therapy. My body was raw with chronic pain. I was told I was in the body of an ill 80-year-old, and there was nothing anyone could do. Most therapies were too much for me, even acupuncture. I could hardly handle a single needle.

As I started with the craniosacral sessions, I found myself immediately going into deep imagery as my body processed and released. My body would drop in temperature to the point where my teeth would chatter like a helicopter after every session, and it took me a while to warm-up.

I recall one session in which I saw that I was deeply encased with thousands of layers of chains. In between the chains was thick, black sludge.

As the treatment session progressed, I felt the chains recede, releasing the great weight. The black sludge started to recede as well. Freedom and re-birth. That session changed my life because I released the chains of pain that had me tied down for years. I realized the gift was that I was continuing to find myself and continuing to let go of all the layers that was hiding who I really am.

Retrieving Fragments

Years later I had another dream of my ex; this time in the dream we had a child together. He wanted to take our child. I was against it. I was angry and non-trusting. It was awful timing because I had a big evening ahead and would be on-stage to do a performance. He said he would bring our child back that evening. I unwillingly let them go. All I could think of was that I would never see him or our child again. I got out on-stage and looked into the audience, but he was nowhere to be found. Panic settled in my stomach and heart. I kept up the performance and continued to scan the room. Nothing. I was finishing my performance when he showed up with our child. I went running toward them, and he willingly handed over our child. I felt that this was a return of my innocence. This was another gift and fragment of me that I was able to reclaim.

Shortly after this dream, I realized that climbing the corporate ladder wasn't for me. It didn't nourish my soul, no matter the experience or the money. It was nice for a while, and then the shiny toy turned dull and tarnished. I had absolutely no idea where to go next. Divine guidance landed in my lap.

I worked with a life coach who helped me to see what I couldn't and pulled out the realization that had made no sense to me previously. That realization was that I was to be a healer and own my own healing center. That sounded great, but now what?

I researched different modalities and decided craniosacral was a definite must-have in my repertoire since I received such life-transforming experiences from it. I then discovered Bowen Therapy, which also changed my life, and then Reiki.

I am continuously reminded that when I leap, I will be caught with open arms. The chaos we think we might be attracting might make it appear that we are falling, but I have been reminded that in order to take the power back, I must dive-in and trust.

Through my journey, I have discovered that I need to learn things the hard way, with hard knocks. Not everyone needs to have such extreme experiences to wake-up. I'm aware that I needed to go there in order to expand as my best self. It took a lot of organizing to get me into some of those lessons, and a lot of hard work to get back on-track with the lessons-learned and accepted.

I now grab life by the mane and ride it all the way to the end. With no regrets. Age has nothing to do with wisdom.

When I first met my most vulnerable self, I didn't think I liked her. I thought she was weak, sad, and alone. I now understand that she is powerful, strong, bold, tenacious, brilliant, beautiful, emotional, wise, compassionate, limitless, and expansive. She is only weak when I hide her. She is only sad when I do not allow her to stand. She is only alone when I do not empower her to be alive. I embrace her; she is the most powerful part of me.

I am in perfect alignment with each and every experience that I co-create. I choose to live now, loving what is and more of what I love becomes my experience. I no longer need to live in the past. I recognize the past as a catalyst; I have great gratitude for my story. It moved me forward into the full expression of who I am: a healer, body-whisperer, teacher, speaker, and author, all in service to you.

You are whole, perfect, and complete just as you are. At every stage in life you are exactly where you need to be. If you weren't you would be having a different experience and that experience would be perfect. But this experience, in this very moment, is exactly where you need to be and it is perfect for you.

Whatever has been created to this point is in alignment with who you are. No matter where you are (even if at a fork in the road, do you turn right or left or decide to turn around and go back to where you came from?), it is all as it is meant to be. With just that mustard seed of faith alone, your life will positively change as did mine.

Dixie Bennett is a luminary leader in the healing arts of Bowen Therapy, CranioSacral & Somato Emotional Release, Reiki Master & Teacher, Evolutionary Life Strategist, Public Speaker, and Author. Through her own evolution of 3 near death experiences, self-discovery and healing, Dixie left 16 years in industries such as retail and oil and gas behind to pursue her passion and purpose of helping others realize that they do not have to live with chronic pain.

Each and every one of you has a story that started the day you were born. Each experience of love, hurt, bullying, anger, success, failure, loss, fear, joy, frustration is all unique to you. Each decision you've made has created the evolution of you, your story, it brought you here to this exact moment. Dixie calls it the Evolutionary Edge, where nothing is yet written, we can create whatever is to happen next.

When working with Dixie, she can see the unseen threads (your experience) woven together that create the physical experience of your life. Over time when these issues have not been dealt with they can cause issues in your tissues, which can lead to dis-ease or critical illness. Dixie helps you get to the CORE of your pain, find your VOICE, stand in your POWER and helps you realize that you can CREATE whatever is to happen next, opportunities are LIMITLESS and you can live a MAGICAL life.

Dixie lives in Calgary, Alberta Canada where she has a full-time successful practice called Stillpoint Bodyworks. She loves to give a heart-felt hug, develop her spirituality, travel, network, connect, mentor and teach. She is continuously expanding herself with personal development. You can also find her performing 6 bass in a local steel drum band called Calysto Steel Band.

Dixie may be contacted at: www.stillpointbodyworks.ca
Facebook: StillpointBodyworks & Dixie Bennett
Twitter: @SPbodyworks
LinkedIn: Dixie Bennett

Closing Meditation

Kathryn Yarborough

We are thankful to all our contributors who have shared their very personal stories, wisdom, guidance, gifts, and expertise with us and the world! Each and every story lovingly supports the fact that—"You are Whole, Perfect, and Complete: Just as You Are." Our goal is to aid other souls find the pathway to who they really are and who they are meant to become on the journey of life. We thought it would be helpful to conclude this book in the same shining light as it was begun with a meditation to bring together on a deeper level all the knowledge and experiences shared in these pages We are grateful to Kathryn Yarborough for this closing meditation. A free download is available at www.youarewholeperfectandcomplete.com —Carol Plummer and Susan Driscoll

"Hello, friend, and welcome. I'm Kathryn Yarborough, and I am going to take you on a journey of remembering that you are already whole, perfect, and complete. So, join me in getting comfortable, and bring your awareness to your breath. And if you're willing, soften or close your eyes, so that you can really go inward.

And feel the breath, come in and go out. Noticing how miraculous it is.

That without even thinking about it, just noticing this breath, this life-giving breath, flows in and flows out.

And become aware of your lungs; how your lungs receive this air. And as you exhale it sends out the air that is not needed; the carbon dioxide that goes out on the exhale. Experiencing how your lungs expand on the inhale. Soften in and contract on the exhale. You don't have to think about that; you can just notice it. You don't have to make that happen. You are already created, whole, perfect, and complete in this way.

The oxygen is pulled out of the air through your lungs and flows into your blood system, and gets carried around your entire body. It's happening right now. It's going to all the different muscles and organs and bones in your body. Every part of you that needs that oxygen...

You don't have to figure it out. You don't have to fix it. You don't have to make yourself anything other than what you are. You are already whole, perfect, and complete. You were created by this great One, that we are all a part of. You are the thing Itself; you are the creation of It; you are a part of It, and this great One is already whole, perfect, and complete as you are. And all of Its creations are just as miraculous as you are. So, just breathe, aware of this incredible chemistry that is going on in your body without any effort on your part that sustains your life.

And become aware of your skin. This skin, this covering that covers every part of your body. Around your toes and your feet; around your legs; the skin that covers, through your pelvis and your buttock, and your belly and your back and your chest. Aware of the skin that covers your arms and hands and fingers, and your shoulders and your neck and face; your head. Aware of how this skin, this organ...skin is an organ. It is already perfect; it is whole, perfect, and complete. Just as it was created by something way more intelligent than anyone of us. As you breathe, and feel, and sense your skin...

Aware. It contains you. It contains your physical self.

I mean, how cool is that? Breathe… Relax. And now become aware of your brain in your head. Aware of how your brain is even processing the sound of my voice and turning it into understandable ideas. And guiding you through an experience. Your brain is doing that. Breathe… Relax. And become aware of how miraculous your brain is. And at the same time it's hearing my voice; it's monitoring your breathing, so you get the right amount of oxygen, compared to the carbon dioxide that you're releasing out.

It's reminding your blood to continue to pump. It's guiding your stomach and digesting the food you ate earlier today. Your brain is doing all of that, without you having to do anything. Your brain has helped you to remember countless pieces of information. Learned concepts, and remembered places and people you know. It's like a computer's memory, way beyond what our computers do even. Breathe and relax, as you appreciate, you.

Your brain. Breathing, and relaxing. Bring your awareness to your heart. In the center of your chest. Actually that is your heart area. Your heart is slightly to the left. Be aware of your heart; the seed of love. Some people would say the second brain.

Your connection with others. And be aware that the heart is a muscle; an organ that pumps the blood, all through the body; continuously.

And how it is whole and perfect and complete, already. You don't have to do anything to fix your heart. It is a miracle, like you. You are a miracle, an incredible combination of atoms and cells, protons, electrons, neutrons, and hydrogen cells, and oxygen cells, and all kinds of things that have come together that makes you.

Breathe. Aware of the miracle that is you. Whole, perfect, and complete.

Just as you are. And become aware of all the muscles, like the muscles that move your legs. And the muscles that move your stomach and your back, and the muscles that move your arms. And with those muscles, your arms move, your legs move; you can walk.

You were created knowing how to do this.

Your body instinctually learned how to walk, how to lift your arm. It just happened. And these muscles fire, and relax, and do all these cool things, so that you can move and interact in the world. Walk and run, and drive a car, and cook dinner, and hug your loved ones. All of these things you can do because your muscles just function.

Aware of the miracle that is you, as you breathe and relax. And is there any other part of your being that you are just aware of how miraculous it is? How whole, perfect, and complete it is. Like how your taste buds can taste different foods, or your stomach that digests foods, or sexual organs that give you pleasure, or bring forth another life.

If you are a woman or a man who helps to create another life—this is so beautiful. Or maybe there are other aspects of you; maybe you have an innate gift. A talent, a creative aspect, or a capacity to learn things, a way of listening that who you are, that is just who you are.

Breathe and relax. Aware of the creation that is you, the gift that is you. Aware that you are already whole, perfect, and complete, just as you are. And there may be some part of you that goes, "Oh, and I want to learn in this way; and Oh, I want to grow in this way; and Oh, there's this other thing that I could do differently in life."

You might have a thought: "Oh, but I didn't do that well. Or Oh, I messed up with that…" Or find some physical flaw, that you would call a flaw. As you breathe and relax… I invite you to just pull out any of those thoughts if you have them.

And hold them, hold them one at a time in your hand, like those flowers in summer that you can put into your hand, and blow on and just flies away. I invite you, with each and every thought that you have, that is anything other than you are whole, perfect, and complete, right now. That you just put that thought into your hand, hold it with tenderness and just gently blow on it and let the air just take it away.

Let it return that thought to all of existence, to be digested, processed, and transformed.

As you focus on the wholeness of you, the perfectness of you, the completeness of you, just as you are, in this moment... Everything about you... Whole, perfect, and complete.

The miracle that is you... Breathe deeply. Aware of this breath. This miracle breath. For as long as you are breathing, you will be in this physical form. A creation of this great One that we are all a part of. Aware of your breath, deep breath.

Aware of the miracle that is you. Whole, perfect, and complete.

Namaste, my friend."

In her "Getting Present" programs, **Kathryn Yarborough** helps folks heal the split between the Divine and everyday life issues (like money). She has helped thousands of people with her signature "5-step breath practice." Before creating online programs, Kathryn had a private practice as a manifestation coach, integrative breathworker, and dance/movement therapist. Find her at www.FlowingWithChange.com